GUIDE TO THE

ROYAL ARCH CHAPTER

JEWISH HIGH-PRIEST IN FULL SACERDOTAL ROBES

GUIDE

TO THE

ROYAL ARCH CHAPTER

A COMPLETE MONITOR
WITH FULL INSTRUCTIONS IN THE DEGREES OF

MARK MASTER, PAST MASTER,
MOST EXCELLENT MASTER AND ROYAL ARCH

TOGETHER WITH THE

ORDER OF HIGH PRIESTHOOD

HISTORICAL INTRODUCTION, EXPLANATORY NOTES,
CEREMONIES, INSTALLATION

Illustrated

By

JOHN SHEVILLE, P.G.H.P.

and

JAMES L. GOULD, P.G.H.P., 33°

MACOY PUBLISHING & MASONIC SUPPLY CO., INC.
RICHMOND, VIRGINIA

Entered according to Act of Congress, in the year 1867, by the
MASONIC PUBLISHING AND MANUFACTURING CO.,
In the Clerk's Office of the District Court of the United States for
the Southern District of New York.

ISBN-0-88053-021-9

Printed in the United States of America

TO THE

M∴ E∴ OFFICERS AND MEMBERS

OF THE

GENERAL GRAND CHAPTER

OF THE

UNITED STATES OF AMERICA

𝕿𝖍𝖎𝖘 𝖁𝖔𝖑𝖚𝖒𝖊

IS

FRATERNALLY DEDICATED

BY

THE AUTHOR

PREFACE

THE unexpected favor with which the appearance of the "Manual of the Chapter" was greeted has induced the author to comply with the frequently expressed desire for the publication of that little work in a larger form, better suited to the use of the older members of the Fraternity. The original work was presented to the Royal Craft, in the hope that it might call attention to the ancient ritual of the Chapter Degrees, in what may be properly called the American Rite. The text of that work has been carefully preserved, and such explanatory notes have been added as seemed to be necessary to render the present volume not only a complete Text Book of the several degrees according to the ancient ritual, but also a Guide for every Companion to a proper understanding of the ceremonies and symbolism of the Capitular degrees.

The author has consulted all the works of previous writers on the subjects investigated, that were accessible, and especially the standard works of JOSEPHUS, PRIDEAUX, OLIVER and MACKEY. He would also take this opportunity to acknowledge his indebtedness for valuable suggestions to a number of his Masonic friends and correspondents, among whom he would particularly mention: Ill.·. JOHN SHEVILLE, his co-laborer in the preparation of the original text of the "Manual of the Chapter," whose knowledge of Masonic ritualism is unsurpassed by any Companion whose acquaintance he has ever made; M.·. E.·. LUKE A. LOCKWOOD, Esq., the accomplished Grand High-Priest of Connecticut; R.·. W.·. CHAUNCEY M. HATCH, Grand Lecturer of the Grand Lodge of Connecticut; Ill.·. ROBERT MACOY, of the city of New York; E. G. STORER, the venerable Past Grand Secretary of the Grand Chapter of Connecticut; and the late ANTHONY O'SULLIVAN, Grand Secretary of Missouri, in whose recent death, the author lost a valued friend and counselor, as did all who knew him.

The work was prepared for the press by the author, in the brief moments snatched here and there from the never-ending cares and labors of his profession, at times but illy suited to successful literary effort. He is not so presumptuous as to hope that it will be found free from imperfections; but, trusting it may cheer the way and strengthen the resolution of some seeker after Light, as taught in the sublime ritual of Capitular Masonry, he submits the present volume to the charitable judgment of the Royal Arch Craft of the Country.

JAMES L. GOULD,

MARCH, 1867.

Bridgeport, Ct.

PREFACE TO THE MANUAL OF THE CHAPTER

Remove not the ancient landmark, which thy fathers have set.—Prov. xxii. 23.

AT a time when the Masonic Fraternity of the country is zealously seeking to discover the "Ancient Landmarks," now almost obliterated by the tide of innovation which has been sweeping over the "old paths" for half a century, it is deemed unnecessary to offer any apology for presenting to the Craft a "Manual" designed to point out the old work.

This little volume is intended to supply a constantly increasing demand for a Monitor of convenient size, devoted exclusively to the Chapter Degrees, and bearing to them the same relation that the several recent reprints of WEBB's Monitor do to the Symbolic Degrees.

An acquaintance with zealous and intelligent Companions of the mystic-tie, more or less extended into every jurisdiction, and a somewhat general personal observation of the work as performed in the different sections of the country, have made known the existing defects and discrepancies in the same, and the wants of the Fraternity in this respect. A thorough knowledge, derived from unquestionable authority, of the *old ritual*, and the present English system, as well as of the different rituals in vogue in the United States for the past thirty years, acquired by earnest study and by several years of constant and *practical* "work in the quarries," has enabled the authors to compare the ritual as practiced in the last century with these later systems, and by this means, to supply, as they believe, a Manual that will "prove of essential service to the Craft" in retracing their steps to the old and tried paths.

The published works of PRESTON, WEBB, TOWN, ROLLIN, DALCHO, SAURIN, OLIVER, HARRIS, BRADLEY, and numerous others, together with many old and valuable unpublished manuscripts of these and other Masonic celebrities of the last century, have been diligently compared in the preparation of this work, and the authors have no hesitation in averring that the arrangement of its several parts is in accordance with the oldest and best system of work in use before the hand of modern innovation and so-called improvement had been laid upon the Lectures and Work of the Chapter Degrees.

Trusting that a Fraternity, whose distinguishing characteristic is *Charity*, will overlook the faults and imperfections that may be discovered in the "Manual," it is submitted to the Companions of the Royal Art in the hope that it may afford useful instruction to those who are seeking after light, and thus lead to a better understanding of the sublime and beautiful ritual of Royal Arch Masonry

JOHN SHEVILLE,

Jersey City, N. J.

JAMES L. GOULD,

Bridgeport, Ct.

SEPTEMBER, 1864.

CONTENTS

INTRODUCTION.. 9
   History of the English Royal Arch...................... 11
   Dermott's Degree...................................... 11
   Dunckerley's Degree................................... 17
   The Union... 24
   Present Status of the English Royal Arch............... 28
   The Royal Arch of Ireland and Scotland................ 32
   Introduction of Masonry into the United States......... 34
   Early History of Royal Arch Masonry in the United States.. 37
   The American Ritual................................... 41
   Symbolism of the Chapter Degrees...................... 43

FOURTH DEGREE—MARK MASTER............................ 47
   History... 48
   Officers.. 50
   Symbolic Color.. 51
   Opening... 52
   Ritual.. 53
   Reception... 61
   Jewel of a Mark Master................................ 65
   Jewish Half Shekel.................................... 67
   Working Tools of a Mark Master........................ 70
   Charge to the Candidate............................... 73
   The Parable... 77

PAST MASTER.. 81
   History... 82
   Officers.. 85
   Symbolic Color.. 85
   Opening... 86
   Ritual and Reception.................................. 87
   The Giblemites.. 87
   Charge to the Candidate............................... 92
   Closing... 94

CONTENTS

MOST EXCELLENT MASTER............................... 95
    History... 96
    Officers.. 98
    Symbolic Color............... 98
    Opening.. 99
    Ritual...101
    Dedication of the Temple.............................104
    Historical Summary..................................119
    Charge to the Candidate.............................125
    Closing...126
    History of King Solomon's Temple.....................128
ROYAL ARCH...131
    Officers...132
    Jewels and Clothing.................................136
    Opening...138
    Charge at Opening...................................139
    Reception...141
    The Ark of Safety...................................162
    The Ark of Alliance.................................163
    The Ark of Imitation................................164
    The Signet of Truth............................. ...164
    The Ark of the Covenant.............................170
    The Pot of Manna....................................173
    Aaron's Rod...174
    The Book of the Law............. 174
    The Shekinah and the Bathkoll.......................182
    Royal Arch Ode......................................183
    Lecture...186
    Charge to the Candidates............................206
    Closing...208
ORDER OF HIGH-PRIESTHOOD.................................209
    Officers..212
    Reception...215
    Closing...227
CEREMONIES OF THE ORDER.................................231
CHAPTER JEWELS..265
MASONIC DOCUMENTS.......................................267

FOREWORD

The more I read, the more amazed I become. And it doesn't really matter what I read—novels, biographies, histories, magazines, manuals, "how to" books, whatever—I find the more things change the more they actually stay the same. If this appears to be a contridiction, think about it. You, too, will be just as amazed.

So it is with this *Guide to the Royal Arch Chapter*. Since its publication in 1864, and its enlarged edition in 1867, Royal Arch Masonry has changed. So has all of Freemasonry and its many offshoots. Yet, when we read what Companions Gould and Sheville wrote well over a hundred years ago, we cannot help but feel it was written but yesterday. The ritual is much the same; the principles are still the same.

Royal Arch Masonry is still divided into four parts—Mark Master, Past Master, Most Excellent Master, and Royal Arch. At least this is the way most of the jurisdictions divide it. Two don't, however. Virginia and West Virginia (whose original Chapters were chartered by Virginia) add the Cryptic Degrees—Royal and Select Master. These are conferred before a Mason receives the Most Excellent Master Degree. In all other jurisdictions the Cryptic Degrees are conferred under the authority of a Grand Council of Royal and Select Masters.

It is interesting to note that more and more jurisdictions are holding combined annual meetings of the Grand Chapter and Grand Council. Several have considered seriously merging into two groups. But, as yet, this hasn't happened. Historically, however, the Council Degrees do take place prior to the events depicted in the Most Excellent and Royal Arch Degrees. This is the way they are arranged in Virginia and West Virginia. The Capitular Masons in these two jurisdictions are also Cryptic Masons. The High Priests of the Chapters are also Thrice Illustrious Masters. And so it is with the Grand officers.

The authors cover the history of each of the Capitular degrees well. Little more has been discovered concerning them during the century since the book was first published. However, the history of the Mark Master (or Mason) Degree in England is most interesting.

In 1856 the United Grand Lodge of England, somewhat reluctantly, agreed "the degree of Mark Mason or Mark Master is not at variance with the Ancient Landmarks." It agreed to permit the degree to be conferred "by all warranted Lodges under regulations suggested by the Board [of General Purposes], approved and sanctioned by the M.W. Grand Master." The Mark Degree was considered by the Board a part of the Fellowcraft Degree. This wasn't acceptable to those who felt the Mark Degree was too important to be a part of another degree. So, a Grand Mark Lodge was founded.

The Grand Chapter of Scotland considered the Grand Mark Lodge of England illegal. Scotland continued to warrant Mark Lodges in England. When condemned for this action, Scotland asked "the United Grand Lodge and the English Supreme Grand Chapter" whether or not "they were prepared to sanction the working of the Mark degree in" England. The two English bodies hemmed and hawed. Finally, they decided NOT to recognize the Grand Mark Lodge or the working of the Mark Degree, even if it was attached to the Fellowcraft Degree.

According to *Grand Lodge 1717-1967*, the history of the Grand Lodge of England, "the Scottish Grand Chapter also declined to recognize the English Grand Mark Lodge." This occurred in 1856. The historian in 1967 wrote: "So far as the Mark degree is concerned United Grand Lodge remains the odd man out." Yet—*The Grand Lodge of Scotland Year Book* has listed for many years "The Grand Lodge of Mark Master Masons of England and Wales." It carries a complete list of the Grand Officers. It was carrying this recognition at the time the English historian wrote that England was "the odd man out."

In 1931, the Irish Grand Lodge adopted the following: "Pure Ancient Masonry consists of the following Degrees and no others, viz.—The Entered Apprentice, the Fellow Craft, the Master Maon and the Installed Master, but the Degrees of Royal Arch and Mark Master Mason shall also be recognized so long as the Supreme Grand Royal Arch Chapter shall work only those two Degrees in the form in which they are worked at the passing of this Law."

The reluctant wording is strange. Freemasons in Ireland had been working in the Royal Arch Degree, or some semblance of it, for almost two hundred years when the new law was adopted. The first printed reference that we know about took place in 1743. A newspaper recorded that a Master of a Lodge was preceded by "the Royall Arch carried by two Excellent Masons." This was a report on a Masonic function at Youghall. In 1744, Dassigny's book was published with an item reading: "I am informed in that city [York] is held an assembly of Master Masons under the title of Royal Arch Masons." In the 1750's Lodge minutes contained many references to the Royal Arch Degree. The first being recorded in the Lodge at Fredericksburg, Virginia, on December 22, 1753.

For more years than anyone can record, a mark (a simple symbol) has been used to tell one man's work from another. All types of marks have been found on the stones of buildings of centuries ago. It was but natural for an organization basing its symbolism on the operative masons of hundreds of years ago to adopt the symbolism of the mark for one of its important degrees. A mark of some type was a necessity when most men could neither read nor write. It readily identified the workman. It continues to be used in industry even today. But how much more pride the workman would take in his production if he had to inscribe his product with his own mark. As in the days of the mark, each man would be accountable for his own part of the whole.

In *The Pocket History of Freemasonry* (another excellent book), Pick, Knight and Smyth record several items which indicate the Mark Degree, and possibly the Royal Arch, was known in the 1720's. They report *A Mason's Examination*, written in 1723, had the following:

> If a Master Mason you would be
> Observe you well the Rule of Three;
> And what you want in Masonry
> Thy *Mark* and *Maughbin* make thee free.

The Free-Masons, 1722-23, wrote satirically:

> They then resolv'd no more to rome,
> But to return to their own Home;
> Tho' first their Signs and Marks did frame,
> To signify from whence they came.

In *The Freemasons; an Hudibrastic Poem*, also from the 1722-23 era, is found:

> A Mason, when he needs must drink
> Sends letter without Pen and Ink
> Unto some Brother, whos at hand
> And does the message understand;
> The Paper's the Shape that's square,
> Thrice-folded with the nicest care.

These tid-bits indicate that the Mark Degree was known as early as the publication of the *Constitutions of Freemasonry* by Dr. James Anderson. They also prove that a *Master Mason* was not unknown. This is contrary to the arguments of many historians who believe the Master Mason Degree was an "afterthought."

In England the Cryptic Degrees consist of others not covered in this area in the United States. Not only the Royal Master and Select Master are under the control of a Grand Council, so are the Most Excellent Master and Super-Excellent Master. The latter two come under Royal Arch Masonry in the United States.

The authors mention St. Andrews Chapter in Boston. They don't note that it was from this Chapter an historical event took place. In 1797, a meeting was held out of which grew what is now the General Grand Chapter, Royal Arch Masons, International. All the Grand Chapters in the United States have joined this organization except Pennsylvania, Texas and Virginia as of this writing. Over the years it has developed into a service association for Royal Arch Masonry. Over the past ten years it has extended its areas of service to include many modern methods of teaching. It is to the Grand Chapters what The Masonic Service Association of the United States is to the Grand Lodges.

Unlike the MSA, however, it is truly international. Several Canadian Grand Chapters are members; so are Chapters of Grand Chapters in Austria, Greece, the Canal Zone, Taiwan, Korea, Japan, Puerto Rico, among others. Royal Arch Grand Chapters exist in Hawaii and Alaska and belong to the General Grand Chapter. There are no Grand Lodges for the latter. They come under the jurisdiction of California and Washington, respectively.

There are many organizations that have attached themselves to Ancient Craft Masonry. It is interesting to note that only one was sanctioned by the United Grand Lodge of England. The second article in the union of the two remaining rival Grand Lodges in England in 1813 declared:

> It is declared and pronounced that pure Antient Masonry consists of three degrees and no more, *viz* those of the Entered Apprentice, the Fellow Craft, and the Master Mason, including the Supreme Order of the Holy Royal Arch.

This book, *Guide to the Royal Arch Chapter*, will give you an excellent start in learning the history and ritual of the Royal Craft. Read it. Enjoy it. Study it. You will be the beneficiary.

ALLEN E. ROBERTS

Highland Springs, Virginia
July 4, 1980

INTRODUCTION

THE antiquity of Freemasonry is generally conceded by all, whether friend or foe; and while some have asserted that "from the commencement of the world we may trace the foundation of Masonry,"* others have deduced its rise at a later date, from the societies of operative Masons and cathedral builders of the middle ages † and still others, preferring a middle ground, derive its origin from the building of Solomon's Temple at Jerusalem. Whatever be the date of its establishment almost all writers are agreed in assigning to the Order an antiquity whose years cannot be definitely measured. Nor is it necessary that we should be able to state its age with precision.

The Order does not depend on its antiquity for its value to the world. Were it but the creation of yesterday this fact would not impair the force of its solemn obligations, diminish its claims upon the good-will of mankind, nor lessen in any degree the sublimity and importance of its teachings. The great popularity of Freemasonry among the good and great, its acknowledged age, its inherent vitality, and its long existence against the combined attacks of religious fanaticism, bigoted intolerance, and blind prejudice, while other human societies have faded away and are forgotten, may indeed serve to convince the world that it has within it the elements of Truth and Virtue; may indeed prove to the candid mind that the Order has been in a special manner watched over and protected by Divine Providence; but to the intelligent Mason these things in themselves are of little worth. He regards the Order as the custodian of great and sublime truths, and loves it for what it is, and not simply for what it may have

* Webb's Monitor.   † Steinbrenner's Origin.

been in the past. He follows its teachings because they lead him upward and onward to a higher and better condition.

Freemasonry has been defined by an eminent American writer,* to be "the most perfect and sublime institution ever formed for promoting the happiness of individuals or for increasing the general good of the community." It has also been said to be a "beautiful system of morality vailed in allegory and illustrated by symbols." This definition of the institution has been generally considered as more especially applicable to the first three degrees, which have been called *par excellence* "Symbolical Degrees;" but, when properly understood and conferred, the Chapter Degrees are equally entitled to the name. Indeed they have a higher claim to the title, because the symbolism of the first six degrees in regular and successive steps, bears the same relation to the Grand Omnific Symbol of TRUTH brought to light in the Royal Arch Degree, that the shadow does to the substance.

The system or ritual of the first three degrees which are the foundation of all Masonic science is essentially the same in all nations and climes, but differences have always existed in the higher degrees as practiced in different countries. It may be owing to this cause that few, comparatively speaking, Royal Arch Masons have understood the full import of the symbolism of the Chapter Degrees; and hence most of our Masonic writers and teachers have been contented with giving necessary instructions for the use of the ritual and ceremonies of the Order. The only work published in this country professing to teach the symbolism of these degrees is Dr. A. G. MACKEY's excellent one, entitled "The Book of the Chapter." This distinguished author has accomplished much good by drawing the attention of the Royal Craft to some of that sublime symbolism which is the glory and beauty of the institution. It may now be said that never before in the history of the Order was there so general a demand among intelligent craftsmen for light on these important subjects. To obtain, however, anything like a correct knowledge of the Royal Art it is necessary to understand something of the con-

* Dr. Dalcho. Orations, p. 7.

dition of the Order at the time of its introduction into this country. To do this we must study the rise and progress of Royal Arch Masonry in the British Isles and to some extent on the continent of Europe. It is therefore proposed to give a concise history of the origin of the Royal Arch and appendant degrees in those countries, as contained in the valuable works of Dr. OLIVER and other historians.

HISTORY OF THE ENGLISH ROYAL ARCH

DERMOTT'S DEGREE

AT what time Freemasonry was introduced into England, or by whom, it is now utterly impossible to tell. It is true, there exist many traces of it at an early period; but the first authentic account of it is the history of the assembly of Masons at York A. D. 926, at which EDWIN presided as Grand Master. From this memorable convention originated the well-known title of Ancient York Masons. At this assembly many old writings were produced in the Greek, Latin, and other languages, from which the Constitutions of the English Lodges were derived. By virtue of the charter granted by ATHELSTANE all the Masons of the kingdom were convened, and a Grand Lodge was established for their government. The history of this Grand Lodge for many centuries is involved in very great obscurity, on account of the destruction, in the year 1720, of many valuable papers and records, by over prudent brethren,* who, fearing the effect of their publication, took that means to prevent it. It is frequently alluded to, however, and continued to exist until some years after the revival, as it has very properly been called, which took place A. D. 1717. At that time it bore the title of "The Grand Lodge of all England," though in fact it exercised no jurisdiction in the south of England. Indeed it would appear that the Grand Lodge at York was little more than an annual assembly of Masons, whose main usefulness consisted in its being the conservator of the primitive Gothic Constitutions and Charges.

* Dr. George Oliver. Origin of the Royal Arch.

A. D. 1717 only four lodges existed in the south of England. On St. JOHN the Baptist's day, in that year, an annual assembly or feast was held for the first time in many years, by the members of those lodges, a Grand Lodge formed under the title of "The Grand Lodge of England," and ANTHONY SAYRE, Esq., was elected Grand Master of Masons. Previous to this time there were no stated or chartered lodges; but a sufficient number of Masons, met together in a certain district, having among them a Master Mason, had ample power to make Masons, without warrant or charter. It was now determined, however, by the new Grand Lodge that this right should be restricted to certain fixed lodges, regularly constituted and chartered by the warrant of the Grand Master approved by the Grand Lodge. But this right to make Masons must be understood to apply only to Entered Apprentices; for the Old Regulations say that "Apprentices must be admitted Fellow-Crafts and Masters only here" (that is in Grand Lodge) "unless by a dispensation from the Grand Master."*

From this it is evident that few of our ancient brethren ever progressed farther than the first degree, which is corroborated by the fact that Entered Apprentices were then members of the Grand Lodge.† In early times, indeed, no one was called a Master Mason until he had become Master of his Lodge.‡ This rule was modified by a new Regulation adopted November 22, A. D. 1725, which ordained that "The Master of a Lodge with his Wardens, and a competent number of his Lodge, assembled in due form, can make Masters and Fellows at discretion."

About this time many other new Regulations were proposed and adopted, which had, and still have, great influence on the Order. First in importance among these was the one allowing the admission of members without regard to occupation or pursuit. Previous to this era the society was composed mostly of operative Masons, with an occasional exception in favor of men distinguished for rank, scientific attainments, or position in civil life, or those who had rendered some eminent service

---

* Old Regulations. Art. x.   † Old Regulations. Art. xxxix.
              ‡ Old Charges. Note to Art. iv.

to the Craft. In order to increase its membership and extend the influence of the Order, the proposition was agreed to that the privileges of Masonry should no longer be restricted to operative Masons, but men of all trades and professions should be admitted to the rights and benefits of the institution on being regularly approved. From this point the Fraternity rapidly acquired popularity and influence. Men of rank and position sought affiliation with the Order, and there came knocking at its doors men of talent and learning. These men applied themselves to the study of its symbols and allegories, and by their labors the dust and rubbish of centuries were removed from the foundation of the old Temple of Operative Masonry, and the new Temple of Speculative Masonry was reared in all its beauty and grandeur, to bless the world in which it was erected.

But this did not satisfy the selfish purposes and ambitious designs of some, who had sought and unfortunately obtained admission to the Order. These men, failing to secure at once the full measure of their ambition, soon became disturbers of the peace and harmony of the Fraternity, as many others have done since, for similar reasons. Hence arose the famous schism among the English Masons, which, continuing for seventy years, has filled the Masonic world till this day, and probably for all time to come, with those differences in rituals, the efforts to remove which have exhausted the ingenuity of man. This schism originated* with some unruly spirits, who, being exceedingly anxious to obtain the Master's degree, prevailed on some inconsiderate Master Masons to open an illegal Lodge, and to raise them to that sublime degree. This was done without the authority or sanction of a warrant, and in direct violation of the Regulation adopted by the Grand Lodge at the revival. At length the facts became known, and complaints were preferred against the offending brethren at the Quarterly Communication of the Grand Lodge in June, A. D. 1739. The schismatics, being joined by others of like character, in defiance of the Grand Lodge opened Lodges in

---

* Dr. Oliver. Some account of the schism, etc. The student who wishes to thoroughly understand this subject should read Dr. Oliver's work.

various parts of London. The Grand Lodge of England now expressly ordered the regular lodges not to admit the seceders as visitors or to countenance or acknowledge them in any way whatever, at the same time adopting as a means of prevention, the systems being the same, a slight change in the forms of recognition. * The seceders at once seized on this circumstance with exultation, accused the Grand Lodge of having deviated from ancient usage and violated the Landmarks, and made it a pretext for stigmatizing the regular Grand Lodge and its adherents as *Modern* Masons. They at the same time appropriated to themselves the exclusive and honorable title of "*Ancient York* Masons." Taking advantage of this popular cry they organized a Grand Lodge† and by their zeal soon gained a wide popularity. Persons of rank were induced to enroll themselves under their banner; and as a means to extend their popularity, they professed to confer benefits and reveal secrets to their initiates not understood by the "Moderns," or adherents of the regular Grand Lodge.‡ They at the same time asserted that the latter did not possess the true "Master's part," or third degree. In the year 1756 LAURENCE DERMOTT§ published his Ahiman Rezon, and therein boldly affirmed that "Ancient Masonry consists of four degrees, the three first of which are those of the Entered Apprentice, the Fellow-Craft,

---

* Noorthouck. Const. p. 240. "To accomplish this purpose more effectually, some variations were made in the established forms."

† The date of the organization of this body has been variously stated. Dr. Mackey, in his Lexicon, gives the date as 1739. Pierson, in his Traditions, gives it as having occurred about 1753. Preston asserts that the seceders continued to hold their meetings without acknowledging a superior until the year 1772, when they chose for their Grand Master the Duke of Athol, then Grand Master elect of Scotland. Sandys, in his "Short View," says they (the Ancients) established their Grand Lodge in London in 1757. In certain testimony taken by commission in England, for use in the New York difficulty some years since, Bro. White, at that time the venerable Grand Secretary of the Grand Lodge of England, says, under oath, in answer to a question, that the Athol or *Ancient* Grand Lodge was formed in 1752. This ought to settle the question.

‡ Ahiman Rezon, pp. 30, 70.

§ Laurence Dermott was an Irish Mason of ability, who affiliated with the so-called Ancients, and was for many years their Grand Secretary. He was afterward the Deputy Grand Master of that body, and to his zeal and talents the *Ancients* owed very much of their prosperity and influence.

and the sublime degree of Master; and a brother being well versed in these degrees, and otherwise qualified as hereafter will be expressed, is eligible to be admitted to the fourth degree, the Holy Royal Arch. This degree is certainly more august, sublime, and important than those which precede it, and is the summit and perfection of Ancient Masonry."*

The earliest reference to the Royal Arch as a separate or fourth degree that I have met is the following from Dr. FIT-FIELD D'ASSIGNEY, published in 1744. The brother says: "Some of the Fraternity have expressed an uneasiness at the Royal Arch being kept a secret from them, since they had already passed through the usual degrees of probation; but I cannot help being of the opinion that they have no right to any such benefit, until they make a proper application and are received with due formality as having passed the chair and given undeniable proofs of their skill."

It is well known by all Masonic students that originally the essential or grand feature of the present Royal Arch Degree was given as a concluding section or completion of the "Master's part." The loss and recovery were so arranged as to follow each other in the same ceremonial. This was undoubtedly the case at the time of the revival, A. D. 1717.

This is conclusively shown by the consideration of the following facts. The first warrant for opening a Lodge in France was granted in 1725 by the Grand Lodge of England to Lord DERWENTWATER and others; and Dr. OLIVER asserts that he has in his possession a French floor cloth of about that date in which the true M. W. is to be found in its original place. Again, the early lectures in use at the time of the revival show conclusively that the Master's degree was then complete in itself.†

Soon after the revival, in 1720, ANDERSON and DESAGULIERS were authorized to revise the lectures. Their revision continued in use until about A. D. 1732, when MARTIN CLARE was authorized to prepare a new revision. Neither of these contained any evidence of a fourth degree.

* Preamble to the original laws of R. A. Degree.
† Lectures of Sir Christopher Wren.

After a full and careful study of the subject, Dr. OLIVER asserts that the earliest mention of the Royal Arch which he can find is in the year 1740.* DERMOTT confesses that the Royal Arch was first practiced in England by the so-called Ancients.† The separation of its concluding portion from the ancient Master's degree, and its erection into another grade or degree, was unquestionably the work of the schismatics. This must have been done between the years 1740 and 1744, and circumstantial evidence would seem to fix the time at or very near the former year.

The *Ancients* having been effectually excluded from the lodges adhering to the Grand Lodge of England, by the adoption of the slight change in the ritual before mentioned, resolved on retaliation. In order to render the schism more complete, and also make amends for their outlawry by the constitutional Grand Lodge, they determined to mutilate the third degree, and from its concluding portion establish a fourth grade, which they called the Holy Royal Arch.

They undoubtedly obtained the idea of this change, and also of the title which they gave the new degree, from Chevalier RAMSAY,‡ who visited England in 1740, and attempted to induce the Grand Lodge of England to adopt his new inventions.§ His

---

* Dr. Oliver. Origin of English Royal Arch, p. 19.

† Ahiman Rezon, p. 114.

‡ Ramsay was born at Ayr, in Scotland, in 1686, and died in France in 1743. He was a man of extensive learning, and a faithful follower of the fortunes of the Pretender; and, it is said, attempted to make Freemasonry subservient to the interests of the house of Stuart. He advanced the theory that the institution arose in the Holy Land during the crusades, as an Order of Chivalry, and originated several new degrees based upon that theory. Among these were three degrees called Scotch Mason, Novice, and Knight of the Temple. In 1728 he also introduced another grade known as Ramsay's Royal Arch. This degree is not the Royal Arch of England, Ireland, or the United States, and is more properly termed the "Arch of Enoch."

§ The date of this attempt of Ramsay is differently stated. Dr. Mackey, in his Lexicón, gives the date as 1728. Dr. Oliver, in his "Revelations of a Square," states the origin of Ramsay's Degrees to have been in 1725, and the same author, in his "Origin of the English Royal Arch," uses this language: "In 1740 he came over to England, and remained in this country more than a year," etc. In another place Dr. Oliver says Ramsay's Degrees were originated in 1728. A. T. C. Pierson, in his Traditions, gives the date of Ramsay's Royal Arch "about 1740, and further says that "about A. D. 1740 Chevalier Ramsay appeared in London."

schemes being rejected by the constitutional Grand Lodge,* he without doubt made overtures to the Ancients, which were more successful. By a comparison of the ritual of RAMSAY'S degree with the earliest ritual of the Royal Arch of DERMOTT, as practiced by the Ancients, it is apparent that DERMOTT and his colleagues must have had a knowledge of the former in constructing their own degree. The learned Dr. OLIVER indeed asserts his belief that in the earliest arrangement of the English degree the details of RAMSAY'S degree formed one of the preliminary ceremonies.† Nothing is therefore more probable than that DERMOTT made use of RAMSAY'S degree as the foundation on which to construct his own.‡ This belief is confirmed by many esoteric reasons, which cannot be written.

Having thus briefly traced the origin of DERMOTT'S degree, or the Royal Arch of the *Ancient* Masons, used by them until the union between the Grand Lodges in 1813, we will recur to the introduction of the degree among the *Moderns*.

DUNCKERLEY'S DEGREE

THE Grand Lodge of England for many years after the origin of DERMOTT'S degree knew nothing of the Royal Arch, and continued the practice of the first three degrees, including the brief completion of the third degree. In the year 1755 it was currently reported among the brethren that some of the members of Lodge No. 94 had been on the continent and there witnessed extraordinary manifestations in Ancient Masonry, which that Lodge had agreed to practice every third lodge night. This Lodge being composed mostly of members who had been affiliated with the *Ancients*, though then acting under a charter from the Grand Lodge of England, was not in the best repute; which gave currency to the report. The Deputy Grand Master, Dr. MANNINGHAM, at once visited the Lodge, and there learned that this pretended *Ancient* Masonry was

* Dr. Oliver. Origin of English Royal Arch, p. 18.

† Dr. Oliver. Origin of English Royal Arch, p. 19, and note.

‡ That Dermott was the master spirit in its fabrication is fairly to be inferred from his well known ability and position among the Ancients, and also from the fact that he never denied its authorship when charged with it.

nothing more than a mixture of what is now known as RAM-
SAY's Royal Arch with DERMOTT's degree, the principal feature
of which was a transfer of the real Landmark of a Master
Mason to a new degree, which was unknown and unrecognized
by the Grand Lodge of England.*

At the ensuing Grand Lodge, March 20, 1755, Dr. MAN-
NINGHAM communicated a statement of these irregularities,
when it was unanimously resolved—

"That the meetings of brethren under any denomination
of Masons, other than as brethren of this our ancient and
honorable society of Free and Accepted Masons, is inconsistent
with the honor and interest of the Craft, and a high insult on
our Grand Master, and the whole body of Masons."†

This appears to have been the first intimation that the
Constitutional Grand Lodge had ever received in regard to
the innovations made by the *Ancients*, and the language of
the resolution it will be observed is exceedingly guarded—a
good example for more modern times. However, the Lodge
No. 94 persisted in holding the obnoxious meetings, and at
the next quarterly communication of the Grand Lodge a vote
was passed erasing that Lodge from the list of regular lodges.
From these facts it is evident that the Royal Arch, in the
form of a separate degree, was at that time wholly unknown
to the *Moderns*.

It soon became, from this action of the Grand Lodge and
the contumacy of Lodge No. 94, a subject of discussion and
controversy. Something of the feeling thus engendered may
be seen in the following circumstance: In 1758 an *Ancient*
Mason applied to the *Moderns* for pecuniary relief, and the
Grand Secretary of the Grand Lodge in reply stated: "Being
an *Ancient* Mason, you are not entitled to any of our charity.
The *Ancient* Masons have a Lodge at the 'Five Bells' in the
Strand and their Secretary's name is DERMOTT. Our society is
neither *Arch, Royal Arch*, nor *Ancient*, so that you have no right
to partake of our charity."‡ From this it is apparent also that

---

* Dr. Oliver. Revelations of a Square, p. 296.
† Minutes of Grand Lodge, 1755.
‡ Ahiman Rezon. Introduction, p. xi.

the Moderns so late as 1758 had not adopted the new degree. About this time,* however, the Rite of Perfection arose in France, and the Royal Arch of that rite, known as "Knight of the Ninth Arch," soon superseded the degree of Chevalier RAMSAY, and may have had some influence in molding subsequent events. About this time a man named THOMAS DUNCKERLEY appeared among the Masonic celebrities of the eighteenth century.† He was a person of rare talents, and exerted during his career a great influence upon the Order, as will be seen. He is described by Dr. OLIVER as "the oracle of the Grand Lodge, and the accredited interpreter of its Constitutions."‡ DUNCKERLEY was authorized by the Grand Lodge somewhere about A. D. 1770⅔ to construct a new code of lectures by a careful revision of the existing ritual, which last was based on the lectures of Dr. MANNINGHAM‖ and MARTIN

---

* Dr. Oliver says in this year (1758) arose the Rite of Perfection, in which he is followed by several other writers, among whom is Pierson; but Dr. Mackey (Lexicon, p. 344,) makes the date to have been four years earlier. From manuscripts in my possession I am inclined to think its origin must have been still earlier. Great numbers of degrees were originated about the middle of the eighteenth century, which are now entirely obsolete, and whose names even are nearly forgotten.

† Thomas Dunckerley is said to have been an illegitimate son of George II. He is described as possessed of a most brilliant intellect. The first public mention of his name I have met, is in connection with the delivery of an address or charge at Plymouth, in 1757. He was appointed Provincial Grand Master for Hampshire in 1766; and for his zeal in the Royal Art, the Grand Lodge resolved that he should rank as a Past Senior Grand Warden. He was Master of a Lodge in 1770, and is said by Pierson (Traditions, p. 322,) to have been Grand Master. But this is probably a mistake as I can find no record of the fact. He is said by Oliver to have been Grand Superintendent and *Past Grand Master* of Royal Arch Masons for the county of Bristol and other counties, under the patronage of the Duke of Clarence, and also Most Em. and Sup. Grand Master of Knights of R. C.; Templars, K. H., etc., of England. Dr. Oliver states that he introduced a revised lecture into the Military Degrees which was in use many years under the name of "Dunckerley's Sections." He died at Portsmouth, England, in November 1795, having been honored and esteemed by all who knew him.

‡ Dr. Oliver. Revelations of a Square, p.90.

§ Steinbrenner. Origin of Masonry, p. 159. Dr. Oliver. Revelations of a Square, p. 91.

‖ It is impossible to give the date when the lectures of Dr. Manningham were promulgated. It must have been somewhere between 1745 and 1755. They never entirely superseded the lectures of Clare.

CLARE.* DUNCKERLEY was a person well fitted for that task. "His views of Masonry were liberal, and he despised sectarian controversy. He frequently visited the *Ancient* Masons' lodges for the purpose of ascertaining what was the actual difference between the two systems, as LAURENCE DERMOTT, in the Ahiman Rezon, had confidently boasted of the superiority of their mode of work over that recommended by the legitimate Grand Lodge; and he carefully culled its flowers, and transplanted them into Constitutional Masonry; for he actually found amongst the *Ancients*, to his undisguised astonishment, several material innovations in their system, including some alteration of the Old Landmarks, and a new application"† of an important item in the third degree. He at once determined to introduce the essential features of this novelty into his own revision of the lectures.

Divesting the DERMOTT degree of many crudities, and in fact substantially rearranging it, he rewrote its lecture, adapting it to his craft lectures, and presented the whole to the Grand Lodge. He had executed his task so well that the Grand Lodge at once adopted his revision of the lectures, the Royal Arch included, without amendment or alteration, and enjoined its practice on all the lodges under its jurisdiction.‡ But Dr. OLIVER regrets that DUNCKERLEY did not still further improve the ritual of the Royal Arch Degree, from the materials which he derived from the *Ancients*, observing, with much force, that he could not have failed to see their incongruity.§ It must be remembered, however, that even the attempt to introduce the Royal Arch at all into the ritual of the *Moderns*

* Martin Clare remodeled the then existing lectures about the year 1732. His system was an amplification and expansion of the previous systems. His version of the lectures is said to have been so judiciously drawn up that, in the language of Oliver, "its practice was enjoined on all the lodges under the Constitution of England, and all former lectures were abrogated and pronounced obsolete. In his lectures we find the first allusion to the symbol of the *point within a circle*, though the point itself had been briefly mentioned in the lectures of Anderson.

† Dr. Oliver. Revelations of a Square, p. 90.

‡ Dr. Oliver. Revelations of a Square, p. 91. Steinbrenner's Origin, etc., p. 160.

§ Dr. Oliver. Insignia of the Royal Arch, p. 11.

was a bold step, and one which would have utterly ruined the Masonic influence of a weaker man. As it was, it required all DUNCKERLEY's own influence, supported by the patronage of the Duke of Clarence, to carry the project through the Grand Lodge. For although it was adopted by that body by a large majority, yet it met vigorous opposition from the minority.

DUNCKERLEY's degree was given as an additional *Master's part*, or, in other words, was simply an amplification or expansion of the original completion of the third degree.* It involved however a further removal of the true M. W. than had been usual, which the older members conceived to be such an innovation that they bitterly opposed the adoption and use of the ritual.

It was not until A. D. 1779 that the new arrangement became generally acquiesced in, as we shall see.

Other additions to the ritual were made by DUNCKERLEY in this system of lectures, a description of which is foreign to our present purpose; but we may say, in passing, that among these novelties were "the theological ladder with its three rounds of Faith, Hope, and Charity," and also "the lines parallel" as symbolic of the two Saints John, this last, by the way, being an innovation which should have never gained currency in a universal institution.

A. D. 1772 PRESTON† published in London the first edition of his work entitled "Illustrations of Masonry by WILLIAM

---

* Dr. Oliver, in a note on page 91 of his Revelations of a Square, says, "I have in my possession a copy of the R. A. Lecture which was introduced into Grand Lodge on the above occasion. It is a curious and interesting document, as constituting a fair evidence of the nature of R. A. Masonry at its commencement in 1740."

† William Preston was a Scotchman by birth, and a man of marked ability. To his labors as a ritualist and historian Masonry is much indebted. He came to London in 1760, and soon after was initiated in a new Lodge working at the time under a dispensation from the *Ancient* Grand Lodge. Having made the acquaintance of James Heseltine, afterward Grand Secretary of the *Moderns*, he became doubtful of the legitimacy of the *Ancients*, and was induced to connect himself with a regular Lodge under the Grand Lodge of England. From this time his advancement in the Order was rapid until he came to exert an influence second to no other person. [See Stephen Jones' Biography of Preston.]

PRESTON."* At this period a literary taste was arising among all classes of society, and its influence began to be felt upon the Masonic Fraternity. A general desire for a more polished ritual was the natural consequence; and hence a revision of the lectures was again demanded, if the Order would meet the exigencies of the times. PRESTON set himself earnestly at work to prepare for this labor, the necessity of which had made itself manifest to his active mind. He sought information from every available source, compared all the existing rituals, and at length produced what is known the world over as the "Prestonian Lectures." These lectures were used by the dependencies of the Grand Lodge of England until the Union A. D. 1813.†

About the same time another Masonic light was beginning to shine. I refer to WILLIAM HUTCHINSON, who published in 1775 his first edition of "The Spirit of Masonry," a work of much merit.‡ The reader of that book will be struck, however, with the fact that the work contains scarcely a vestige of an allusion to the Royal Arch.§ The same is true of PRESTON'S "Illustrations;" for the slightest allusion to that degree does not appear in the edition of that work published in 1781.

* This work went through many editions, and was universally conceded among the regular Masons to be the standard book of the Order, even so late as the Union in 1813. It was first reprinted in America in the year 1804, and I have before me an edition printed in London so late as 1840. The Freemason's Monitor, published in 1797, by Webb, was a reprint of Preston's work to a very large extent, so far as the first three degrees. Webb's lectures in those degrees were only a revision of the Prestonian system. Preston divided the first lecture into six sections, the second into four, and the third into twelve sections. Webb simplified this construction, but undoubtedly derived most of his ritual from the system of Preston. It has been said that Webb visited England to obtain information from Preston himself, but this is a mistake.

† Dr. Oliver asserts (Revelations of a Square, p. 127,) that Preston first presented his lectures to a meeting of Grand Officers and other eminent brethren held at the Crown and Anchor Tavern in the Strand, on Thursday, May 21, 1772.

‡ William Hutchinson was an attorney of extensive practice, and was greatly respected for his literary acquirements and his cultivated mind. He was for many years Master of a Lodge; and died April 7, 1814, at the advanced age of eighty-two years.

§ Steinbrenner (Origin, etc., p. 161,) says: "It is supposed that Hutchinson and Preston at length united," and "that the lectures of the former were merged into those of the latter."

though the next edition (1788) contains several Royal Arch odes by DUNCKERLEY and others.

The Royal Arch Chapter as a separate body, but under the authority of the Grand Lodge, was established in London some time prior to 1780,* and yet it did not receive the slightest notice from PRESTON in his edition of the next year, a fact which would seem to warrant the conclusion that even then the Royal Arch was not in very high repute among the *Moderns*.

At this time the title "Excellent" was applied to the degree and its possessors.†

A brother who had received the degree was said, in the ritual and also in the certificates issued in those days, to have been "passed" to the "Supreme Degree of Excellent R. A. Mason."‡

The first Book of Constitutions of the Royal Arch was issued in 1786 by the "Supreme Grand Chapter." The regulations contained in this Book of Constitutions were agreed to, however, May 10, 1782, and it is said were drawn up by DUNCKERLEY.§

It will be borne in mind by the reader that the *Ancients* had at this time a Grand Chapter and a system of laws for the government of the Royal Arch, and that the DERMOTT lectures were used by them without having undergone any essential change.

* William Sandys, in his "Short View," states that this occurred in 1777 or thereabouts. Dr. Oliver, in his "Origin of the English Royal Arch," gives it as his opinion that the body referred to was established in 1779. Clavel contends that the Royal Arch Degree originated in 1777; but he probably refers to the establishment of the Royal Arch Chapter.

† Dr. Oliver. Origin of the English Royal Arch, pp. 24–27.

‡ As these certificates show how the chapter was then held (at the time of the formation of the Grand Chapter), it may be interesting to transcribe one. "We the three Chiefs and Scribe, whose names are hereunto subscribed, do certify that in a Chapter of Holy Royal Arch, convened and held under the sanction and authority of the worshipful Lodge No.——, our beloved brother A. B. having delivered to us the recommendation of the Lodge —— hereunto subjoined, and proved himself by due examination to be well qualified in the several degrees of Apprentice, Fellow-Craft, and Master Mason, *and having passed the chair*, was by us admitted to the Supreme Degree of Excellent Royal Arch Mason." From this it appears that "passing the chair" was then a prerequisite for the Royal Arch Degree.

§ Dr. Oliver says these Regulations were agreed to by the *constitutional Grand Lodge*. Origin, etc., p. 9.

Thus the Royal Arch Degree was practiced under these two distinct and antagonistical jurisdictions until the union of the two Grand Lodges in 1813.

It was during this unsettled period that the Royal Arch was generally introduced into America, and as might be expected the same difficulties and disturbances were transplanted into this country as already existed in England. Before our investigation of the American system, however, it will be more in accordance with our design to complete our consideration of the English Royal Arch.

THE UNION

THE election of the Duke of Athol as the Grand Master of the *Ancients* at once gave rise to the closest alliance between them and the Grand Lodges of Scotland and Ireland, inasmuch as that nobleman was then also the Grand Master of Scotland. This cordiality between these several Grand Lodges induced the *Moderns* to make an effort in the year 1801 to bring about a union of their Grand Lodge with that of the *Ancients*, or Athol Masons, as they now began to be called. This effort, however, had no immediate effect, not being met with a corresponding spirit by the *Ancients*.

The next step toward a reunion of the Craft originated in 1803, with the Earl of Moira, the Deputy Grand Master of the Grand Lodge of England. At the grand festival of St. ANDREW, holden at Edinburg, Nov. 13, in that year, Lord MOIRA, who was present as an invited guest, introduced the subject of the schism in England, and explained the action of the Grand Lodge of England in the premises. This led to mutual explanations between the Grand Lodges of England, Scotland, and Ireland, and a most friendly intercourse between these influential bodies. * This good feeling was still further confirmed by the election of the Prince of Wales as Grand Master of Scotland, he already holding that honorable position in the Grand Lodge of England. This alliance between these several Grand Lodges, and their earnest wishes publicly expressed that the schism might be healed, seem to have

* Oliver's edition of Preston, p. 277.

made a strong impression on the *Ancients*, who, becoming
alarmed lest this strong coalition should overthrow their
authority and influence, now became exceedingly anxious to
complete the reunion of the two bodies. This disposition
was undoubtedly still further increased by the fact that all
the differences between the two systems in the United States,
where both had been early planted, were already settled or
in process of settlement. The difficulties constantly arising
among the Craft, from the existence of the two organizations,
had become so irksome that all right-minded men were
anxious to see the schism brought to an end, and the most
influential members of the Order upon either side interested
themselves to promote a settlement of the trouble. But it
was necessarily a work of time. Prejudices of long standing
were to be removed, personal animosities of the most bitter
character were to be mollified, opinions of the most diverse
natures were to be harmonized, and hence it will not surprise
any one familiar with the Masonic history of the time, that
the desired object was not consummated until 1813. It will
be remembered also that each of the opposing Grand Lodges
was a large body, composed of the first talent in England,
and presided over by distinguished noblemen.* In addition
to this it must also be borne in mind that each Grand Lodge
had a large amount of property, and a charity fund managed
by its board. All the intricate questions growing out of these
circumstances had to be fairly adjusted to meet the views and
sanction of men who had been but recently inflamed with
hatred toward each other. In such a state of things the
object could only be attained by the exercise of charity,
patience, and forbearance. In the year 1809 the constitutional Grand Lodge met the overtures of the Ancients by
passing a resolution, "That it is not necessary to continue in
force any longer those measures which were resorted to in or

* "In 1717 there were only four lodges in the south of England; but in 1730
they had increased to 245 registered lodges; in 1767 there were 416; in 1795 we
find 542; in 1804, 600 on the books of the Grand Lodge of England, beside about
300 lodges of Ancient Masons; some of them being in foreign countries, and
others itinerant; in 1811 the number of both amounted to nearly 1,000." Oliver.
Historical Landmarks of Freemasonry, p. 215.

about the year 1739, respecting irregular Masons; and we, therefore, enjoin the Lodges to revert to the ancient landmarks of the society."* An occasional Lodge was then appointed, called the Lodge of Promulgation, as a preparatory step to carrying out the union of the two Grand Lodges.

This concession of the *Moderns* removed the greatest obstacle in the way of the return of the *Ancients*, and was followed, on their part, by the resignation of the Duke of Athol, their then Grand Master, and the appointment of the Duke of Kent to that office. His brother, the Duke of Sussex, was at this time the Grand Master of the *Moderns*, having been elected to that position on the accession of the Prince of Wales to the Regency, and his consequent resignation of the Grand Mastership. Under the skillful direction of these two illustrious brothers the Union was accomplished and finally consummated on St. JOHN'S day, Dec. 27, A. D. 1813.

The original articles for the Union were signed, ratified, and confirmed, and the seal of the respective Grand Lodges affixed Dec. 1, 1813.†

The second of these articles was as follows: "It is declared and pronounced that pure Ancient Masonry consists of three degrees, and no more, viz: those of the Entered Apprentice, the Fellow-Craft, and the Master Mason (including the Supreme Order of the Holy Royal Arch). But this article is not intended to prevent any Lodge or Chapter from holding a meeting in any of the degrees of the Orders of Chivalry, according to the constitutions of the said Orders."

The third article provides that "there shall be the most perfect unity of obligation, of discipline, of working the lodges, of making, passing and raising, instructing and clothing brothers."

* Grand Lodge Minutes, 1809.

† These articles are very interesting, and can be found entire with a description of the rich and gorgeous ceremonies of the reunion in the minutes of the United Grand Lodge, and in Dr. Oliver's edition of Preston's Illustrations. The whole of this interesting history of the formation of the United Grand Lodge should be understood by every Mason. The substance of the second article is still retained in the Constitution of the United Grand Lodge of England.

To accomplish this uniformity the articles further provided for the appointment of nine "worthy and expert Master Masons or Past Masters," from each of the two Fraternities, who should meet and form a "Lodge of Reconciliation," whose duty it should be to prepare the way for the Grand Reunion. This Lodge was also charged with the duty of ascertaining from a comparison of the two systems of work and lectures, and from other sources, what the ancient landmarks and work of the Order was, and directed to communicate the same to the several lodges about to be united. Rev. SAMUEL HEMMING, D.D., was the leading man in this Lodge of Reconciliation, and hence the work and lectures promulgated by the Lodge have been known as the Union or HEMMING Lectures. They were, of necessity from the constitution of the Lodge, a compromise between the systems of PRESTON and DERMOTT, modified by the individual views of the authors of the new system.* Some of the most important symbols and teachings of the Prestonian Ritual are entirely omitted in the HEMMING system, which is now the standard work of the "United Grand Lodge of Ancient Freemasons of England."† The changes thus made in the three degrees would not be considered by American Masons as any improvement on our established modes of work.‡ From what has been said it is apparent that since the revival in 1717 until the Union in 1813, a period of less than one hundred years, the lectures and ritual of English Freemasonry have been authoritatively revised and changed at least seven or eight times, and while the Fraternity of that country have generally observed the binding force of the fundamental landmarks,

* See Dr. Oliver on this subject; also Steinbrenner. Origin, p. 161.

† Dr. Oliver says (Symbol of Glory, p. 100), "Many of the above illustrations were expunged by Dr. Hemming and his associates in the Lodge of Reconciliation, from the revised Lectures; *Moses and Solomon were substituted as the two Masonic parallels, etc.*"

‡ The difference between the *Ancient* and *Modern* systems is stated by Dr. Oliver thus: "The *Moderns*, so-called by the innovators, retained the original system, consisting of three degrees, in all its integrity; the *Ancients*, so-called by themselves, mutilated the third degree by dividing it into two parts, and pronounced in the Book of Constitutions that *genuine Ancient Masonry consists of four degrees.*" Revelations of a Square, p. 299.

yet we are forced to admit that at least in two notable instances
such was not the case.* It further appears that in so far as
the present system adopted by the Grand Lodge of England
differs from the Prestonian Lectures, our English brethren
have a more modern ritual than the American, as the American system is substantially that of PRESTON. Nor does it
satisfactorily appear as has been alleged by a recent author†
that the English ritual is the more intellectual of the two, but
the contrary is undoubtedly the truth. The union of the two
Grand Lodges prepared the way for the union of the two
Grand Chapters, which occurred A. D. 1817. The united
body was at first styled "The United Grand Chapter," but
in 1822 the title of "Supreme Grand Chapter" was resumed.

Thus was brought to an end the English Masonic schism,
out of which grew the Royal Arch, and from whose results
the Masonic Fraternity will probably never recover.

THE PRESENT STATUS OF THE ENGLISH ROYAL ARCH

As before remarked, the Royal Arch system was practiced
as an appendage to the third degree for many years after its
introduction. At that early period any Lodge convened a
Chapter and conferred the Royal Arch Degree under the
sanction of its own charter. Gradual steps were taken in
process of time, however, which little by little separated
Capitular from Lodge Masonry until distinct warrants were
declared to be necessary to authorize the holding of Chapters;
and the Order of the Royal Arch became after the lapse of
many years an independent rite.

The English Royal Arch at present is worked from the
tracing boards of HARRIS, published under the sanction of the
Supreme Grand Chapter, and its ritual is somewhat different
from that in use at the Union in 1817.

According to the Constitutions it appears to be practiced as
a *fourth* degree, although the Articles of Union declare that
Ancient Masonry consists of *three degrees only, including the*
Royal Arch. The Supreme Grand Chapter holds theoretically

---

* For example, the act of 1739 and the separation of the Royal Arch.
† Pierson. Traditions, p. 327.

the position that "the Royal Arch is not essentially a degree, but rather the perfection of the third." In practice, however, the degrees differ in design, in clothing, in constitutions and in color, and the proceedings are regulated by different governing bodies. Dr. OLIVER confesses that this position of the degree is both anomalous and at variance with all the true principles of Masonry;* and while his own opinion seems to be that it should be made a part of the third degree,† yet he candidly admits that there are eminent companions in his own country who adopt the view that it is more properly the seventh degree. In a note in one of his latest works, he uses in this connection the following language: "It is an established doctrine of the Order that while three form a Lodge, and five may hold it, seven only can make it perfect. In such a case there requires an intermediate degree to complete the series; for the *Mark and Past Masters have been already admitted into the Craft Lodges*. This degree, as used by our transatlantic brethren, who are zealous and intelligent Masons, is called the (Most) Excellent Master." In another place the same author observes: "If, however, Freemasonry, in its present form, requires the Royal Arch to be considered as a separate degree, inasmuch as it has acquired the designation of Red Masonry in contradistinction to the three first degrees, which are esteemed blue; and not only possesses detached funds, but is placed under the direction of a different governing body, with a separate code of laws, it will be more consistent with the general principles of the Order, to consider it as the seventh than the fourth; for four is not a Masonic number; and as it is now constituted, some intermediate ceremonies appear to be necessary to connect it with the previous degrees."

This anomalous position of the Royal Arch is perhaps one of the very worst difficulties of English Masonry, and out of it arise many of their troubles. To avoid these, some of the ablest craftsmen of that country are persistently urging the

* Historical Landmarks, vol. 1, p. 469.

† "The Royal Arch is evidently, therefore, to be considered as a completion of the third degree, which, indeed, appears broken and imperfect without it; and *originally was conferred complete at one time in the Grand Lodge only*." Hist. Land., vol. 1, p. 470. Note.

adoption of the system made use of in the United States. It is to be hoped that the efforts of these learned and zealous companions will result in the general adoption of the American ritual, which, in its details and arrangement, is more complete and finished than any other now in use.

By the present English Constitutions, the Supreme Grand Chapter of England does not require the possession of anything more than the Master's degree as a pre-requisite for the Royal Arch. Any Master Mason of twelve months' standing is eligible for the honors of the Royal Arch, although on being proposed and balloted for two negatives will prevent his exaltation. Neither the Mark, Past, or Most Excellent degrees are deemed pre-requisites, though all of them are being conferred to some extent.

The Supreme Grand Chapter allows the Principals of their Chapters to issue a warrant for the holding of Lodges to confer the intermediate degrees. This custom is, perhaps, better than not to have those degrees at all, but our English companions would find it for the advantage of the Order, if their Grand Chapter would at once take those degrees under its government, and incorporate them into its capitular system. Indeed the Past Master's degree has been now firmly established as a separate grade with distinct privileges and badges.* The DERMOTT degree, as practiced by the *Ancients* so early as 1744, required the possession of the Past Master's degree or ceremony as a preliminary qualification, and such continued to be the case until the union of the two Grand Chapters in 1817.†

DUNCKERLEY'S degree seems to have been conferred at first without the requirement of the Chair degree as a preliminary, but, when an independent government was established in 1779, and separate Chapters were held, the candidates, unless they were actual Past Masters,‡ were required to present a dispensation from the Grand Master authorizing them to "privately pass the chair."§

* Dr. Oliver. Origin of the English Royal Arch, p. 40.

† Ahiman Rezon. L. Hyneman's reprint, p. 49.

‡ Dr. Oliver. Origin of English Royal Arch, p. 26.

§ Pierson (Traditions, p. 291,) pertinently remarks: "Where a Grand Master derives his authority to grant such dispensations, or how he became possessed of jurisdiction over '*passing the chair*,' is a problem worth solving."

This dispensation was in practice issued only upon the recommendation* of the Lodge to which the candidate belonged. The possession of the Chair degree was required by the *Moderns* until the Union—and hence the present practice of dispensing with that pre-requisite is a palpable violation of the ancient practice of both sections of the English Royal Arch Fraternity. This innovation has led to much confusion, and should have never been tolerated.

The fact that English Royal Arch Masons had not received the intermediate degrees naturally led to their exclusion from the American Chapters. A case of this kind was brought to the notice of the General Grand Chapter of the United States at its session in 1844, and led to the adoption of a resolution conferring the right upon the several Chapters under its jurisdiction to confer the degrees of Mark Master, Past Master, and Most Excellent Master free of charge, on any worthy Companion Royal Arch Mason from without the jurisdiction of the United States, who had not received those degrees.† The same thing was subsequently incorporated into, and is now a part of, the constitution of the General Grand Chapter.‡

Another anomaly in the English Royal Arch is the making of EZRA and NEHEMIAH to be the cotemporaries of ZERUBBABEL and JOSHUA. The second temple was dedicated in the year 515 B. C.; but EZRA did not go up to Jerusalem until 457 B. C., or seventy-eight years after the return of the Jews under ZERUBBABEL; and NEHEMIAH's government did not begin until twelve years later than this.

Another anomaly in the English ritual is to be found in the names of the first three officers of a Chapter, which are termed

---

* The form of this recommendation was as follows: "*Whereas*, our trusty and well-beloved Brother ———, a geometrical Master Mason, and member of our Lodge, has solicited us to recommend him as a Master Mason, every way qualified for passing the Holy Royal Arch; we do hereby certify that so far as we are judges of the necessary qualifications the said brother has obtained the unanimous consent of our Lodge for this recommendation." This was signed by the Master and Wardens of the Lodge.

† Compendium of Proceedings of Gen. Gr. Chapter, p. 135.

‡ Article III., Sec. 5.

Principals. The first with them is the King, the second is the Prophet or Scribe, and the third is the High-Priest. This is evidently incorrect. *

There are many other inconsistencies which it is not our purpose to discuss. It has been asserted that the American system is inferior to the English, and it has been our design to direct inquiry to a comparison of the two systems, rather than attempt a vindication of the American degrees from the charge.

We will now turn to a brief consideration of the Royal Arch of Ireland and Scotland, leaving the inquirer after truth to pursue this investigation which, at every step, exhibits new phases of interest.

THE ROYAL ARCH OF IRELAND AND SCOTLAND

The capitular system of Ireland is essentially different from any other. It consists of three degrees, the Excellent, Super Excellent, and Royal Arch, as a preliminary step to which the Past Master's degree is indispensable. The first two of these degrees refer exclusively to the legation of MOSES, and are conferred in lodges governed by a Master and Wardens. These degrees, of course, bear no resemblance to the Most Excellent and Super Excellent degrees known in this country. The Royal Arch is given in a Chapter governed by three Principals without names, differing in this respect from the English Chapters.

The ritual of the Irish Royal Arch is based on the discovery of the book of the law as related in 2 Chronicles, chapter xxxiv. verse 14, and hence its date is about 624 B. C. Of course the ceremonies are essentially different from those of other countries. From whence this degree was derived or when it was introduced into Ireland, I am unable to say. A recent writer asserts that no trace can be found of it in Ireland earlier than 1751. The Committee of Foreign Correspondence of one of our oldest Grand Lodges in a recent report make the statement that DERMOTT introduced the Royal Arch into Ireland by conferring the degree on Irish Masons in London.

* See further on this subject under the Royal Arch Degree—title, *Officers.*

This is undoubtedly an error, because there is no resemblance between the Irish degree and that of DERMOTT. This consideration is sufficient to warrant the conclusion that the two systems had an entirely different origin.

Dr. OLIVER expresses no decided opinion on the subject, but says it is doubtful whether the degree existed in Ireland earlier than 1740.

The Royal Arch system of Scotland is still different in its degrees and organization. The Mark and Past Master, which are called "Chair degrees," are indispensable qualifications. Next after these the candidate receives two other degrees, entitled Excellent and Super Excellent, as preparatory to the Royal Arch. In addition to these five degrees, which may be said to compose their Capitular rite, Scottish Chapters also confer on Royal Arch Masons the degrees of Royal Ark Mariner and Babylonish Pass.* As the reader will perceive, the ritual must be essentially different from either of the others that we have referred to. The Mark degree is not the same as the American Mark degree, and the Excellent is given as a preliminary to the departure of the Hebrew captives from Babylon, and is, of course, wholly unlike anything in the American rite. The Royal Ark Mariner and Babylonish Pass are sometimes given in this country as side degrees.

The era commemorated in the Scottish Royal Arch is the same as in the English and American degree.

There has been published but very little authentic information concerning the introduction of the Royal Arch into either Ireland or Scotland, and it is to be hoped that some qualified companion of the Craft in those countries will give the world a history of the origin and early years of the Royal Arch in both countries.

From a comparison of the ritual of the *Ancients*, and those of Ireland and Scotland, it would seem that but little influence was exerted by them upon one another, although such a friendly feeling existed between them for many years.

The earliest mention of the existence of Royal Arch Chapters in Scotland is under the date of 1755 concerning Glasgow

* Gen. Reg. for the government of the Order of R. A. Masons in Scotland, 1845.

Royal Arch, No. 77, and in 1759 concerning Stirling Royal
Arch, No. 93, they undoubtedly being chapters attached to
the lodges bearing those numbers.

The present Grand Chapter of Scotland was not formed
until A. D. 1818.

INTRODUCTION OF MASONRY INTO THE UNITED STATES

THE earliest account of the introduction of Masonry into
the United States is the history of a Lodge organized in
Rhode Island, A. D. 1658, or fifty-nine years before the
revival in England, and seventy-five years before the establishment of the first Lodge in Massachusetts. Rev. EDWARD
PETERSON, in his "History of Rhode Island and Newport in
the Past," gives the following account of this early Lodge:
"In the spring of 1658 MORDECAI CAMPANNALL, MOSES
PACKECKOE, LEVI, and others, in all fifteen families, arrived
at Newport from Holland. They brought with them the
three first degrees of Masonry, and worked them in the house
of CAMPANNALL, and continued to do so, they and their successors, to the year 1742."*

This is, without doubt, the first Lodge ever held in the
limits of the present United States.

The Order was introduced into Pennsylvania in the year
1732, but from what source I have been unable to ascertain.

A warrant dated April 30, 1733, was granted by Lord
MONTACUTE, Grand Master of the Grand Lodge of England,
to HENRY PRICE, Esq., of Boston, appointing him Provincial
Grand Master for New England, with power to appoint his
Deputy Grand Master, and Grand Wardens.   July 30, A. D.
1733, the Provincial Grand Master organized his Provincial
Grand Lodge under the name of St. JOHN's Grand Lodge.
The first act of this body, after its organization, and on the
same day, was the institution of "The First Lodge in Bos-
ton," which was again chartered in 1792 by the name of St.
JOHN's Lodge.   Early in 1734 the authority of Grand Master
PRICE was extended by the Grand Lodge of England over all

* Page 101.

North America, and in pursuance thereof, June 24, in that year, a warrant was issued to BENJAMIN FRANKLIN for what was termed "The First Lodge in Pennsylvania." This was the first warranted Lodge established in that State under the Constitution of the Grand Lodge of England.

At the time of the organization of the St. JOHN'S Grand Lodge in Boston, and for years after, its subordinates did not confer the Master's degree, confining their labors to the first two degrees. Accordingly, in the year 1738, a body called "The Master's Lodge" was organized in Boston, to meet monthly, whose work was exclusively confined to conferring the Master's degree on brethren who had received the two preceding degrees in some one of the other Lodges then existing in the colony.* The ritual used in this "Master's Lodge" was the original "Master's part," practiced by the Grand Lodge of England at that period, including the essential of the Royal Arch, and was, unquestionably, the first use of that ritual in this country.

In the year 1756 a number of brethren, who are said to have been "*Ancient*" Masons, petitioned the Grand Lodge of Scotland, and obtained a warrant for a new Lodge in Boston, to be called St. ANDREW'S Lodge. St. JOHN'S Grand Lodge, conceiving this act of the Grand Lodge of Scotland to be an infringement of their jurisdiction, "refused any communications or visits from such members of St. ANDREW'S Lodge as had not formerly sat in their Lodges." In consequence of this refusal St. ANDREW'S Lodge united with two army Lodges then located in America, one being No. 58 on the registry of England, and the other, No. 322 on the registry of Ireland, in petitioning the Grand Lodge of Scotland for the appointment of a Provincial Grand Master. The Earl of Dalhousie, Grand Master of Scotland, accordingly issued his commission bearing date May 30, 1769, appointing JOSEPH WARREN, afterward known as General WARREN, of revolutionary fame, Provincial Grand Master of Masons, "in Boston, New England, and within one hundred miles of the same." This authority was subsequently extended over the whole continent. Gen.

* Moore's Magazine, vol. 16, p. 135.

WARREN was installed Grand Master, and the Grand Lodge organized Dec. 27, 1769. This body was known as "Massachusetts Grand Lodge." It steadily continued to prosper, discontinuing its meetings only for a short time during the war which soon followed its organization. This Grand Lodge, and its subordinates which it chartered, evidently made use of the ritual of Scotland or that of the *Ancients;* more probably the latter, for the reason that the founders of St. ANDREW's Lodge were *Ancient* Masons, and undoubtedly exercised a controling influence in the Grand Body; indeed, WEBB, writing only twenty-five or thirty years after, says as much. These facts have great weight in the consideration of the early condition of the Order in this country.

The present Grand Lodge of the State of New York was first constituted by a warrant from the Duke of Athol, dated Sept. 5, 1781.

The Grand Lodge of Pennsylvania was first constituted by a grand warrant from the Grand Lodge of England, dated June 20, 1764.

The Grand Lodge of North Carolina was first constituted by virtue of a charter from the Grand Lodge of Scotland, A. D. 1771.

Thus the two systems of work which have been known as "*Modern*" and "*Ancient*" were planted in different States, and from thence were disseminated throughout the country. In some of the States, as in Massachusetts and South Carolina, there existed two Grand Lodges, whose systems were essentially different. Of course the same causes led to the same results in connection with the ritual and organization of the Capitular degrees. Soon after the close of the revolutionary war an earnest effort was made on the part of eminent brethren in different sections to unite the Fraternity in each State under one Grand Lodge, a result which was finally accomplished. The union of the two Grand Lodges in Massachusetts was consummated June 19, 1792, and was followed at intervals by like action in other States.

EARLY HISTORY OF ROYAL ARCH MASONRY IN THE UNITED STATES

AT what time or by whom Royal Arch Masonry as a separate rite was introduced into the United States has never yet been settled. It has been frequently claimed that the first record of its existence in this country is to be found in St. ANDREW's Royal Arch Lodge connected with St. ANDREW's Lodge before mentioned, in the year 1769.* This, however, is a mistake. There was a Chapter held so early as the year 1758, in Philadelphia, which was unquestionably the oldest distinct organization of Royal Arch Masons ever held on this continent, although this was itself held under the sanction of a Master's Lodge warrant.† This was in accord with the practice at that day of all Chapters, and even now Chapters are attached to some Lodge in England, Ireland, and Scotland. It will also be observed that this was prior to the recognition and adoption of the Royal Arch by the Grand Lodge of England, and hence the degree thus early worked in Pennsylvania must have been the DERMOTT degree, or at all events it could not have been DUNCKERLEY's degree, as has been stated by a late author.

The next body of Royal Arch Masons of which we have an account is St. ANDREW's Royal Arch Lodge, before mentioned,

* Moore's Magazine, vol. xii., p. 165. Pierson's Traditions, p. 324.

† The editor of the Masonic Mirror and Keystone, formerly published in Philadelphia, in the third volume, page 15, (January, 1854,) in speaking of this subject, uses the following language: "Philadelphia has the honor of holding the first warrant for a Chapter in the United States; this Chapter is yet in existence, and has never ceased its meetings from the date of its organization, 1758." This statement has never been to my knowledge questioned. The talented and intelligent author of the Report of the Committee on Foreign Correspondence, presented to the Grand Chapter of Missouri in 1855, gives in that report a brief account of this Chapter. He says: "The first Royal Arch Chapter of which your Committee possesses a particular account is that held in Pennsylvania anterior to the year 1758. This Chapter, working under the warrant of Lodge No. 3, was recognized by and had Masonic intercourse with a Military Chapter working under a warrant of Lodge 351, granted by the Athol Grand Lodge, who subsequently approved of its proceedings. Upon like principles other Chapters were formed in Pennsylvania."

organized in Boston, it is said, in 1769.* The ritual used
in this body was certainly that of DERMOTT; and may have
been obtained from the *Ancients* directly or by the way of
Scotland by the brethren of the three Lodges who about that
time petitioned for the Grand Lodge; or it may have been
brought to Boston by one or both of those Army Lodges.
At all events they assisted at the organization of the "Royal
Arch Lodge." And to this connection may be traced the
reason why an *English* Lodge under the *Moderns* should have
united with an Irish and Scotch Lodge in forming a new
Grand Lodge under the authority of the Grand Lodge of
Scotland, in territory in which there was already existing a
Grand Lodge legally constituted by its own mother Grand
Lodge. But when we remember that the Grand Lodge of
England had not yet recognized the Royal Arch degree, nor
authorized its subordinates to confer it, we can readily see
why the Army Lodge under its jurisdiction should have united
itself so closely with St. ANDREW's Lodge. It was evidently
that its members might obtain the new degree.

It will be observed, also, that the degrees then conferred in
St. ANDREW's Royal Arch Lodge were the same in number and
title as those then conferred by similar bodies in Scotland,
and which are now recognized as the constitutional degrees
by the Grand Chapter of Scotland.

In the record of the first meeting the officers are designated
as in a Craft Lodge, but in a subsequent record the first officer
is styled "Royal Arch Master."† The meetings were held in

* In the December number, 1865, of Moore's Freemason's Monthly Magazine,
the editor says: "The records show the existence of the Chapter (then called a
'Royal Arch Lodge') as early as 1768. In the record of the following year we
find the following entry: 'The petition of Bro. William Davis coming before the
Lodge, begging to have and receive the parts belonging to a Royal Arch Mason,
which being read was received, and he unanimously voted in, and was accordingly made by receiving the four steps, that of an Excellent, Super Excellent,
Royal Arch and Knight Templar.' It will be perceived that but one, if indeed
either, of the intercalary degrees, as they are now given, was recognized as
belonging to the Chapter at the date of this record. The Past Master's degree
or ceremony was then given in its proper place; and the Mark degree was
conferred in a Mark Lodge."

† Moore's F. M. Magazine, vol. xii., p. 167.

the lodge-room of St. ANDREW's Lodge, "at the Green Dragon
Tavern." Its work was done under the sanction of the warrant of that Lodge, and it continued thus attached to St.
ANDREW's Lodge certainly until 1790, and probably until the
organization of the Grand Chapter in 1798.* It held its meetings at regular intervals until 1773, when they were suspended
in consequence of the disturbed condition of the country.
In 1789 its meetings were resumed, and curiously enough the
titles of the officers appear in the first record after this re-
sumption, as High-Priest, King, and Scribe. In 1793 the
degree of Mark Master Mason was added to the other degrees
conferred in the Lodge, and in 1794 the body seems to have
assumed the status of an independent Chapter, inasmuch as
it took the name of "St. ANDREW's Royal Arch Chapter."
These changes were due to the transformation then going on
among the elements of American Royal Arch Masonry, consequent on the union of the different systems before mentioned.

Prior to the organization of any Grand Chapters there existed in the city of New York two Chapters, one known as the
Old Chapter and the other called Washington Chapter, the
origin or early history of which has never been published.†
The latter body, Washington Chapter, issued charters to a
number of subordinate Chapters, in which charters it styled
itself "The Mother Chapter." From this body originated
the first Chapters in Rhode Island and Connecticut. The
history of that Chapter, if its early records could be found,
would throw much light upon the condition of Royal Arch
Masonry of that date. As before remarked the first Chapter
in Rhode Island was chartered in 1793 by this Washington
Chapter of New York.

The first Chapter in Connecticut was called Hiram Chapter
No. 1, and located at Newtown in Fairfield County. It was
chartered by Washington Chapter, New York, its charter

* The following is recorded under date of Nov. 25, 1790; "*Voted*, That Bro.
Matthew Groves be a committee to return the thanks of this Lodge to St.
Andrew's Lodge for their politeness in granting us the use of their charter."

† Diligent inquiry has been made for some account of these bodies, but
nothing has yet been found. They never became subordinate to the Grand
Chapter of New York, and must have died out some time subsequent to 1805,
as Webb's Monitor, edition of 1805, alludes to them as then being in existence.

bearing date April 29, A. L. 5791, and is signed by JOSIAH O.
HOFFMAN, H. P. W. C. R. A. M., GEORGE ANTHON, K–g W. C.
R. A. M., and MARTIN HOFFMAN, S–e, W. C. R. A. M.

Five other Chapters were instituted in Connecticut under
the authority of this Washington Chapter as follows:

Franklin Chapter at New Haven, its charter being dated
May 20, 5795;

Solomon's Chapter at Derby, its charter bearing date March
15, A. L. 5796, although its first record is of the date of
December 29, 1795;

Franklin Chapter at Norwich, its charter being dated March
15, 5796, and signed by JOHN ABRAHAM, M. E. H. P., JOHN
LUDLOW, M. E. K., and WILLIAM RICHARDSON, M. E. S;

Van-Den-Broeck Chapter at Colchester, its charter being
dated April 9, 5796; and

Washington Chapter at Middletown, its charter being dated
March 15, A. L. 5796, and countersigned by EZRA HICKS,
Secretary of Washington Chapter.*

These six Chapters made returns, as appears from their
records, to Washington Chapter up to the organization of
the convention of Royal Arch Chapters in the State of
Connecticut.

The first convention of the Chapters in Connecticut was held
on the first Wednesday of July, 1796, at Hartford, in which
all the Chapters above named were represented by delegates,
except Franklin Chapter, at New Haven. A regular organization was perfected and articles of agreement were entered into
for the government of the several Chapters in the State.
Another convention was held October 20, 1796, at New Haven,
of which DAVID BALDWIN was chairman.   The Connecticut
convention met again in May, 1797, and again in October, 1797,
and at this date Bro. JUDD was the presiding officer, and such
distinguished men as EPHRAIM KIRBY and STEPHEN TITUS HOS-
MER were prominent members. The organization was called
"A Convention of Committees of the Chapters of R. A. M.
in Connecticut," and was, so far as I can learn, the first governing body in Royal Arch Masonry organized in the United

* These dates and names are given with the hope that they may lead to the
discovery of the early records of Washington Chapter.

States. The Grand Chapter of Pennsylvania was not established until late in the year 1796, or early in the succeeding year, several months after the Connecticut convention. The first meeting of delegates at Boston, out of which arose the General Grand Chapter, occurred October 24, 1797, almost sixteen months after the organization of the Connecticut convention. In January, 1798, the convention adjourned from Boston, met in Hartford, and organized the Grand Chapter of the Northern States.* The subsequent history of Royal Arch Masonry being accessible in the records of the several Grand Chapters, we do not propose to follow the subject further at this time. If what we have written from the few sources of information which have been accessible shall lead to a fuller investigation, the cause of Royal Arch Masonry will be promoted, and we shall have accomplished our purpose.

THE AMERICAN RITUAL

The ritual of the Capitular Degrees must have undergone many changes during the latter years of the last century. The union of the several Grand Lodges having been accomplished, the attention of the Craft was turned to the work, inasmuch as it was a necessity of that union, that there should be a uniform mode of conferring the degrees. An eminent lecturer in a recent work asserts that "after mature deliberation, it was determined that the principal Grand Officers of the Grand Lodges of the New England States should perform this duty,"† and then the distinguished brother adds: "And, accordingly, about the year 1797 they commenced their labors." Again he says, in the same article: "After the organization of Chapters of Royal Arch Masons and Lodges of Mark Masters, Past Masters, and Most Excellent Masters, it was deemed absolutely necessary to systematize the work and the lectures pertaining to the same, and, accordingly, the

* As will be seen from page 9 of the Compendium of Proceedings of the Gen. Grand Chapter, a strong effort was made to induce the Connecticut Companions to give up their prior organization and unite in the formation of the Grand Chapter of the Northern States, and it will be observed that two of the Con. necticut Companions were chosen officers in that body, viz: Ephraim Kirby Grand High-Priest and Stephen Titus Hosmer Grand Treasurer.

† Jeremy L. Cross. Advertisement to Masonic Text-Book.

same committee which had been appointed for the first three degrees received the Chapter Degrees in charge." It is said that in private conversation Mr. CROSS gave the names of THOMAS SMITH WEBB, HENRY FOWLE, Rev. GEORGE RICHARDS, Rev. JONATHAN NYE, JOHN HANMER, JOHN SNOW, STEPHEN BLANCHARD, and others, as the prominent members of that committee. That some such committee made improvements in the rituals about the time of the organization of the Grand Chapter of the Northern States is possible, but the work in the several degrees had been systematized and made uniform in Massachusetts, Connecticut, Rhode Island, and New York, before 1797. By whom this was done, it is perhaps now impossible to say, but it does not appear that WEBB could have done it. WEBB was not made a Mason until 1792-3, and the first we know of him as a Masonic ritualist is not until his removal to Albany in 1795 or 6. In 1797 he was the High-Priest of Temple Chapter, and, in that capacity, represented that body in the convention at Boston, which prepared the way for the organization of the Grand Chapter. In September, 1797, his Freemason's Monitor was copyrighted; and its preparation must have been the work of the time which intervened between his arrival in Albany and the date of its publication.

But, as we have seen, the Royal Arch ritual must have been substantially the same as now, at the time Washington Chapter of New York chartered the subordinates in Rhode Island and Connecticut, as evidenced by the titles of the officers and expressions used in the early records of those Chapters. Again, we have other undoubted evidence that the ritual had been revised, and a system of work adopted composed of the two principal ones before in use, and that, too, at some period between 1790 and 1795. THOMAS SMITH WEBB, though a young Mason, at once seized upon this system, made such alterations in it as he deemed necessary, and then published its exoteric portions. Hence it came to be known as the WEBB work. To disseminate and give character to this ritual, WEBB conceived the idea of organizing a Grand Chapter, and at once lent all his energies to accomplish his design. That accomplished, it furnished a vehicle to disseminate his work, and he availed himself of the advantage. While he lived, no one questioned his authority, but at his death many of his pupils, ambitious to fill his place in the Fraternity, began to make alterations in his work, until the old time jealousies and discrepancies became multiplied to an almost unlimited extent. For these evils a return to the early American ritual as practiced in the latter part of the last century is the only remedy. Nor do we recommend a blind acceptance of a thing because it is venerable in years. The true standard by which to test Masonic work is this: it should be consistent with itself, in strict agreement with sacred history, and calculated to convey to the initiate great and solemn truths by means of its symbols. If tried by this test, a work is deficient, then no matter what its age, it is not true Masonry; but if in addition to the essential principles above mentioned, it also possesses a venerable past and the sanction of the fathers, then, indeed, we may hold fast to it; and from it derive both instruction and delight.

SYMBOLISM OF THE CHAPTER DEGREES

The late distinguished brother, Rev. SALEM TOWN, has left on record a brief summary of the symbolism inculcated in the several degrees which deserves to be read by every Mason. "The first degree in Masonry," he says, "naturally suggests that state of moral darkness which begloomed our world. On the apostacy of our first common parent, not a gleam of light was left to cheer his desponding mind. Soon, however, the first kind promise was made. Adam was, therefore, in a comparative sense, still in darkness. Such is the very nature of the first degree, that every observing candidate is led to view his moral blindness and deplorable state by nature. Under these impressions he enters on the second degree, which, in view of his moral blindness, he is to consider emblematical of a state of imprisonment and trial. Such was the second state of ADAM. Hence arises the idea of probationary ground. A due observance of all former requisitions, and a sincere desire to make advances in knowledge and virtue, open the way for the reception of more light. Having diligently persevered in the use of appointed means, the third

degree prefigures the life of the good man in his pilgrimage
state. Although the true light has shined into his heart, and
he has experienced much consolation, yet he sometimes wan-
ders into devious and forbidden paths. In the midst of such
trials he resolves to be faithful, and manfully to withstand
temptations. He determines to pursue that sacred trust
committed to his care, and, therefore, endeavors to escape for
his life to the Great Ark of his salvation. In advancing to
the fourth degree, the good man is greatly encouraged to
persevere in the ways of well-doing even to the end. He has
a name which no man knoweth save he that receiveth it. If,
therefore, he be rejected, and cast forth amongst the rubbish
of the world, he knows full well the Great Master Builder of
the Universe, having chosen and prepared him as a lively
stone in that spiritual building in the heavens, will bring him
forth with triumph, while shouting grace, grace to his Divine
Redeemer. Hence opens the fifth degree, where he discovers
his election to, and his glorified station in, the kingdom of
his Father. Here he is taught how much the chosen ones
are honored and esteemed by those on earth, who discover
and appreciate the image of their common Lord. This image
being engraven on his heart, he may look forward to those
mansions above, where a higher and most exalted seat has
been prepared for the faithful, from the foundation of the
world. With these views the sixth degree is conferred, where
the riches of divine grace are opened in boundless prospect.
Every substantial good is clearly seen to be conferred through
the great atoning sacrifice. In the seventh degree the good man
is truly filled with heartfelt gratitude to his heavenly benefactor, for all those wonderful deliverances wrought out for
him while journeying through the rugged paths of human life.
Great has been his redemption from the Egypt and Babylon
of this world. * * * Such is the moral and religious
instruction derived from the order of the Masonic degrees."

The object and aim of all Masonic science is the search
after truth. Divine Truth is symbolized by the Logos, the
Word, the Name; not only as a mere symbol, but as the
sentient, active, creating and preserving power. It was the
Name, or Word, or Logos, that created the world and spake

its teeming life into being. It appeared to ADAM in the garden, and in the form of a glorious Shekinah, expelled him from Paradise. It appeared to ABRAHAM on Mount Moriah; to JACOB in his vision; and to MOSES at the Burning Bush. The search for this Symbol, the study of this Truth, the pursuit of the Word is the object of our labor. To that symbol all the lessons inculcated in the several degrees unerringly point. Through that symbol all the other symbols of Masonry guide us upward to the Creator. The great and sacred NAME which is ineffable and ever glorious, is the grand central symbol of the Order, and the true Mason is he who understands and appreciates this fact; and then makes its legitimate results practical in his life.

In the Entered Apprentice degree the candidate for Masonry is required to declare his belief in the existence of GOD, because no one can with propriety enter upon a search for that which he does not confidently believe to exist. Hence no one can be allowed to take even the first step in Masonry, until he publicly professes his faith in that Great I Am of whom the tetragrammaton is the symbol. The first prayer of the Mason is for the gift of divine wisdom that he may be better enabled to display the beauties of virtue to the honor of that holy name. By his circumambulation he is taught the labors and trials that will beset him in his progress toward the discovery of TRUTH. By the vail of secrecy which is spread around the institution, the neophyte is instructed that the TRUTH he is to search for is enveloped in mystery. The sublime words of the Great Builder: "Let there be light, and there was light," prefigures the mental and moral illumination, the spiritual light which he will receive, who obtains a knowledge of the symbol which we are considering; and the three great lights, now, for the first time, masonically presented to the brother teach him those great lessons that must guide his steps in all the future. So the northeast corner and the memorial for the archives point to the symbol we are considering. In like manner the pillars of Wisdom, Strength, and Beauty point the neophyte forward to that triune word that planned, created, and adorned the universe, while Faith,

Hope, and Charity lead him up the theological ladder to that divine Love which sustains and redeems the world.

The blazing star and the point within a circle are also symbols leading forward the mind of the candidate to the symbol of symbols—the central point around which revolves the whole science of Ancient Freemasonry. In the Fellow-Craft degree, as we enter the middle chamber, we observe the prominent emblem of that degree, the letter G, the English substitute for the Hebrew *yod*, and are taught to do reverence to the NAME, before whom all Masons from the youngest E.·. A.·. to the W.·. M.·. humbly, reverently, and devoutly bow.

Among the orientals the number fifteen was deemed sacred because the letters of the holy name, JAH, were in their numerical value, equal to that number. Therefore, even the winding-stairs, with the fifteen steps, are symbolic of the name of GOD.

In the third degree, the Mason is taught the great truths of the resurrection and life eternal. The whole legend of the degree points to the power, beneficence, and eternity of the deity, and among the symbols we may refer to the all-seeing eye symbolical of the omnipresent deity.

In the Mark Master Mason's degree, the stone set at naught of the builders, which became the chief stone of the corner, the symbol of the white stone, and the *New Name;* in the Most Excellent Master's degree—the key-stone, and the ark of the covenant—all these and many other symbols of the Order, in all the degrees, are but the shadows, the forerunners, the types of the great symbol upon which the whole fabric of Masonry is constructed.

The Mason who does not look beyond the mere forms and ceremonies of the institution fails, utterly fails to realize the import of its teachings. Its sublime truths are indeed mysteries to him. But no brother, and especially no companion, can fail to become wiser and better, if he will pause on his way through the degrees, and deliberately study the allegories and symbols so profusely set before him in Freemasonry. No matter in what direction he may turn, the lessons of truth are set before him on every side, and it only remains for him to study their deep and hidden meaning.

FOURTH DEGREE

OR,

MARK MASTER MASON

HIS degree of Masonry was not less useful in its original institution, nor are its effects less beneficial to mankind, than those which precede it. By its influence each operative Mason, at the erection of the Temple of SOLOMON, was known and distinguished by the Senior Grand Warden. By its effects the disorder and confusion that might otherwise have attended so immense an undertaking was completely prevented; and not only the craftsmen themselves, who were eighty thousand in number, but every part of their workmanship was discriminated with the greatest nicety and utmost facility. If defects were found in the work, the Overseers, by the help of this degree, were enabled, without difficulty, to ascertain who was the faulty workman; so that its deficiencies might be remedied without injuring the credit or diminishing the reward of the industrious and faithful among the Craft.

HISTORY

The origin of this degree has been the subject of much speculation, and is still involved in doubt. Dr. OLIVER says that anciently it was a degree leading to the Master Mason's chair. Many writers have claimed it was formerly a part of the second degree, as the Royal Arch was of the third, and such may have been the case at some early period, but there has been no conclusive evidence of the fact produced as yet. It is perfectly certain that none of the ceremonies now used in this degree belonged to the Fellow-Craft degree, at the revival in 1717. There are two degrees called Mark Man and Mark Master conferred in Europe, but they have but very little resemblance to the American degree. The latter is now being conferred in England by the tolerance of the Masonic authorities, rather than under their sanction. At the first introduction of this degree into this country it was considered a side degree which any three brethren had the right to confer, and it was not until several years had elapsed that the degree began to be regularly conferred in Lodges. Subsequently, however, independent Lodges of Mark Master Masons were held, and even after the organization of Grand Chapters, Lodges were held by separate charters distinct from the Chapters. The loose manner in which the degree was at first conferred in this country necessarily prevented the keeping of records, and hence there is great difficulty in tracing its early history.

The first record of the practice of the degree on this continent, that I have seen, is among the early records of Masonry in Halifax, Nova Scotia. This record bears date Nov. 16, 1784, at which time the degree was conferred by any brother who possessed it, in a Lodge held under the sanction of the warrant of a Master's Lodge.* From these records it further appears that Mark Lodges were regularly held under the sanction of, and annexed to, at least three Lodges in Halifax.

Other Lodges were held in a similar manner, in different sections of America, from the period above mentioned down to the adoption of the degree by the Chapters.

As early as 1786 JOSEPH MYERS deposited in the archives of the Supreme Council of the Ancient and Accepted rite at Charleston, S. C., the ritual of a degree called *Master Mark Mason.* From whence he obtained it, is unknown.† This degree of MYERS was a side or detached degree, and, as such, was given by the Sovereign Grand Inspectors of that rite; and a charter was issued by the Grand Council of Princes of Jerusalem, for a regular Lodge of Master Mark Masons, in Charleston, Jan. 21, 1802.‡ About that time, however, the use of that degree seems to have virtually ceased in consequence of the Chapters assuming jurisdiction of the Mark Master's degree. From a comparison of the rituals of MYERS' degree, and of our present Mark degree, it is evident that they came from a similar source, though there are many

* This first record is as follows: Halifax, 16th Nov. 5784.—Upon application to the Worshipful Bro. Fife, he was pleased to open a Master Mark Mason's Lodge.

W. Bro. Fife, Master, formerly of No. 213 L. Square; Bro. Hall, Senior Warden; Bro. Allen, J. Warden, of Lodge No. 155; Bro. Lewis, Tiler, of Lodge No. 210.

The following brethren received the degree of Master Mark Mason, and made choice of their mark, as follows. Then follow the names, Lodge membership, and marks of six candidates. The record then proceeds as follows: "These brethren having justly paid the demand for such marks, received the same with proper instructions. The business of the night being finished, the Lodge was closed in due form." These records are continued through the two succeeding years.

† Pierson. Traditions, p. 260.   ‡ Address of Supreme Council, Dec. 1802.

essential differences. In the modification of the Chapter degrees, which took place about the year 1792, it is quite probable that the present degree may have been enriched by portions of the MYERS' degree.*

One of the traditions preserved among Masons relates that the degree of Mark Master Mason was instituted seven days after the foundation stone of King SOLOMON's Temple was laid, when the three Grand Masters assembled the Masters of all the Lodges of Fellow-Crafts, and conferred on them this degree. At the same time the Grand Masters established those admirable regulations for the inspection of the materials as they came from the quarries, which so readily enabled the Overseers to detect imperfect work. According to this tradition the degree, at its institution, was conferred not only as an honorary reward for previous industry, skill, and fidelity, and also as an encouragement to persevere in well doing; but it was still further designed as a practical means for preserving due discipline and oversight at the erection of the temple.

OFFICERS

THE regular Officers of a Lodge of Mark Master Masons are:

1. RIGHT WORSHIPFUL MASTER;

2. SENIOR GRAND WARDEN;

3. JUNIOR GRAND WARDEN;

4. SENIOR DEACON;

5. JUNIOR DEACON;

6. MASTER OVERSEER;

7. SENIOR OVERSEER;

8. JUNIOR OVERSEER.

A distinguished American author, after giving a list of the officers as above, inadvertently without doubt,

* Pierson (Traditions, p. 261), claims that the American degree was arranged from that of MYERS.

makes use of the following language: "The degree cannot be conferred when less than six are present, who, in that case, must be the first and last three officers above-named."* According to the ritual of the degree, at least *eight* besides the candidate are absolutely necessary to work; and in most, if not all, of the jurisdictions, this is the settled rule. It should be made the uniform and imperative practice wherever the American degree is conferred.

The officers of a Chapter take rank as follows, viz: the High-Priest, as R. W. Master, in the E.; King, as S. G. Warden, in the W.; Scribe, as J. G. Warden, in the S.; Captain of the Host, as Marshal or Master of Ceremonies, on the left, in front; Principal Sojourner, as Senior Deacon, on the right, in front; Royal Arch Captain, as Junior Deacon, on the right of the S. G. Warden; Master of the Third Vail, as Master Overseer, at the E. Gate; Master of the Second Vail, as Senior Overseer, at the W. Gate; Master of the First Vail, as Junior Overseer, at the S. Gate; the Treasurer, Secretary, and Tiler (and Stewards and Chaplains, if any), as officers of the corresponding rank, and stationed as in a Lodge of Master Masons.

The symbolic color of the Mark degree is purple. The apron is of white lambskin, edged with purple, and the collar of purple, edged with gold.

A candidate receiving this degree is said to be "advanced to the honorary degree of a Mark Master."

Lodges of Mark Master Masons are dedicated to H∴ A∴ B∴

* Dr. Mackey. Lexicon, p. 129.

OPENING

CHARGE TO BE READ AT OPENING

WHEREFORE, brethren, lay aside all malice, and all guile, and hypocrisies, and envies, and all evil speakings. If so be ye have tasted that the LORD is gracious; to whom coming, as unto a living stone, disallowed indeed of men, but chosen of GOD, and precious; ye also, as lively stones, be ye built up a spiritual house, an holy priesthood. to offer up sacrifices acceptable to GOD.

Wherefore, also, it is contained in the Scripture, behold, I lay in Zion for a foundation, a stone, a tried stone, a precious corner stone, a sure foundation: he that believeth shall not make haste.

Brethren, this is the will of GOD, that, with well-doing, ye put to silence the ignorance of foolish men. As free, and not as using your liberty for a cloak of maliciousness; but as the servants of GOD. Honor all men; love the brotherhood; fear GOD.

Or the following may be used:

PRAYER

Father of Mercies, wilt thou, at this hour, put to silence the ignorance of foolish men; and grant that all malice and all guile, and hypocrisies, and envies, and all evil speakings may be removed far from us, that we may, indeed, taste that the LORD is gracious. Make us to be as living stones, tried and accepted of thee, to be built up in that spiritual building, that house not made with hands, eternal in the heavens.

So mote it be.—AMEN.

RITUAL

SECTION FIRST

THIS section explains the preparatory circumstances attending the advancement of candidates, and exemplifies the regularity and good order that were observed by the craftsmen at the building of the temple; illustrates the method by which the idle and unworthy were detected and punished, and displays one of the principal events which characterizes this degree.

*   *   *   *   *   *

Here the initiate is informed of the proper materials
necessary in the construction of the temple; the place
whence they were obtained, and the manner in which
they were inspected, approved or rejected.

The stones of which the temple was constructed were of white
limestone or a species of marble. This material is described as
being soft and easily worked, but hardening by exposure. Recent
discoveries in Jerusalem have left no room for doubt as to the
precise place from whence those immense stones used in the edifice
were taken. A recent traveler thus describes a vast excavation
which had been discovered about two hundred yards east of the
Damascus gate of the city: "This remarkable place, which is
evidently nothing else than a vast under-ground quarry, large
enough, even as far as it has been explored, to have furnished the
materials for the building of the temple, and the walls of Jerusalem,
extends south-east of Mount Moriah in the direction of the Mosque
of OMAR. The roof of this enormous excavation, which took us
about three hours in perambulating, is supported at intervals of
about twenty, thirty, or forty yards, by square, massive, tower-
like bastions or pillars of various hights and dimensions formed

out of the native rock, or rather left there standing by the surrounding parts being cut away. The marks of the chisel on the dry portions of the rock looked as new and fresh as if the workmen had only just retired."

Another traveler says: "I have roamed abroad over the surrounding hills, even to Mizpeh, where SAMUEL testified, and into the long, deep, limestone quarries beneath Jerusalem itself, whence SOLOMON obtained those splendid slabs, the origin of which has been so long unknown." It is quite evident from the discoveries of the last few years that the larger stones of the temple were taken from the immediate vicinity of the edifice. There is every reason, however, to believe, that stones of smaller size and finer quality were obtained from the famous quarries of Zarthan.

*   *   *   *   *   *

Nothing but good work—true work—square work, is wanted for the building of the temple.

*   *   *   *   *   *

Holy Scripture informs us that "the house, when it was in building, was built of stone made ready before it was brought thither; so that there was neither hammer nor ax, nor any tool of iron heard in the house while it was in building."* The traditions of the Order assert that the stones were squared, marked, and numbered in the quarry, so that when they were brought to Jerusalem each part was found to tally with such precision that when finished the temple appeared to be composed of a single stone. In order to fit with so much exactness each stone must have been good work, that is, of good material, and properly wrought and polished; true work, that is, of right dimensions and true to the pattern; square, that is the angles all being exact right angles; and so in the erection of our spiritual temple, we must build with the squared stones which are the perfect actions of a good man's life, of which each brother must contribute his full quota, emblematically wrought, marked, and numbered, until the moral structure is complete—a building not made with hands, eternal in the heavens. In the language of an early writer: "He that is truly square, well polished, and uprightly fixed, is qualified to be a member of our most honorable society. He that trusteth such a person with any engagement is freed from all trouble and anxiety about the performance of it, for he is faithful to his trust; his words are the breathings of his heart, and he is an utter stranger to deceit."

Such must we all be if we would expect to pass the test of the Grand Overseer's square.

The Three Gates

The ancient mythologists divided the future world into two realms, one being the infernal regions, and the other the elysium, or abode of the gods. Each of these was accessible by three gates, through one of which all mortals were to pass after death. In like manner the Jews assigned to their Gehenna three openings or gates, which they supposed were respectively situated in the wilderness, in the sea, and at Jerusalem. Allusions to these gates are frequent in the Scriptures. JACOB said of Bethel: "This is none other but the house of GOD, and the gate of heaven."†

* 1 King, vi. 7.　　　　　† Gen. xxxviii. 17.

The psalmist, in several places, speaks of the "gates of heaven" and the "gates of death." A representation of similar gates is still extant on the triumphal arch of S. Maria Maggiore, at Rome. A symbolical gate-way arched over is placed at the bottom of a geometrical stair-case, another about midway up the ascent, and a a third at the top. These are the gates of heaven, which are expanded to admit all those who have faithfully performed their duty to GOD, their neighbors, and themselves.

At the building of the temple no work was suffered to pass the gates but such as the proper officers had orders to receive, and no craftsman was entitled to wages until his work had been approved. These wise regulations were necessary in order to insure the reception of good, true, and square work only; and by them we are symbolically taught to try all our actions by the square of virtue, that thus being able to exhibit suitable specimens of our. labor on earth, we may be suffered to enter the burnished gates of the new Jerusalem, and prove our right to receive wages by the true token of Faith.

The sixth hour of the sixth day of the week

The Jewish week began with the Christian Sabbath or our Sunday, and closed with their Sabbath or our Saturday. The sixth day of the Jewish week was, therefore, our Friday. The Jews divided their day into twelve hours, commencing at sunrise and ending at sunset. The sixth hour was noonday or "high twelve." The precise time, therefore, alluded to here was Friday noon, when the Craft, in temple times, are said to have been called from labor to refreshment. The labors of the week being thus brought to a close, the faithful, whose work had been approved, at a given signal formed in procession, headed by the J. G. W., and moving to the notes of cheerful music, presented themselves at the proper place to receive their weekly pay. If any one demanded wages when none were due him, he was at once, by the wise precaution of King SOLOMON, detected and made to suffer the penalty of an impostor. So we are here taught the important lesson that we should be particularly careful never to take wages not our due, lest we should wrong a brother by taking that which in God's chancery belongs to him.

*   *   *   *   *   *

The Seventh Day

In six days God created the heaven and the earth, and rested upon the seventh day; the seventh, therefore, our ancient brethren consecrated as a day of rest from their labors, thereby enjoying frequent opportunities to contemplate the glorious works of creation, and to adore their great creator.

Hymn—*Old Hundred*

Another six days' work is done; An-oth-er

Another six days' work is done; An-oth-er

Sab-bath is be - gun; Return, my soul! en -

Sab-bath is be - gun; Return, my soul! en -

- joy thy rest, Improve the day thy God hath bless'd.

- joy thy rest, Improve the day thy God hath bless'd.

In holy duties let the day--
In holy pleasures pass away!
How sweet a Sabbath thus to spend,
In hope of one which ne'er shall end!

* * * * * *

The obligation resting upon Freemasons to remember the Sabbath day and keep it holy is alike recognized and enforced in the great book of the law which lies open at all times upon their altars, and in the traditions and lectures of their Order. They all inform us that the Almighty Builder of the universe having finished the sixth day's work rested on the seventh. "He blessed, hallowed, and sanctified it. He, thereby, taught man to work industriously six days, but strictly commanded him to rest on the seventh, the better to contemplate on the beautiful works of creation—to adore him, as their creator—to go into his sanctuaries, and offer up praises for life and every blessing he so amply enjoys at his bountiful hands."

The first hour of the first day of the week

* * * * * *

At the building of the temple, according to tradition, the craftsmen arose with the sun and pursued their labor with the same regularity that marks the course of that luminary. The time designated by the "first hour of the first day of the week" was the hour after sunrise on the day succeeding their Sabbath, equivalent to what is now our Sunday morning. This was the hour when the craftsmen in the quarries of Zarthan and in the forests of Lebanon resumed their weekly labor.

SECTION II

Illustrates the foundation and history of the degree, and impresses upon the mind of the candidate, in a striking manner, the importance of a strict observance of his obligation to be ever ready to stretch forth his hand for the relief of indigent and worthy brethren. A variety of interesting circumstances connected with the building of King SOLOMON's Temple are detailed, and the marks of distinction which were in use among our ancient brethren are explained.

RECEPTION

* * * * * *

* * * * * *

The following Scripture passages are appropriately introduced:

The stone which the builders refused is become the head stone of the corner.

Did ye never read in the Scriptures, The stone which the builders rejected, the same is become the head of the corner?

And have ye not read this Scripture, The stone which the builders rejected is become the head of the corner?

♫ ♫

What is this then that is written, The stone
which the builders rejected, the same is become
the head of the corner?

*   *   *   *   *   *

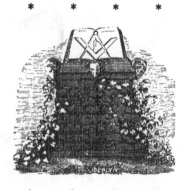

*   *   *   *   *   *

He that hath an ear to hear, let him hear

*   *   *   *   *   *

As the Fellow-Craft degree refers to and describes the five senses
of human nature, so in this degree two of them, Hearing and
Feeling, are particularly alluded to.

In the language of the old lectures: "Hearing is that sense by
which we distinguish sounds, and are capable of enjoying all the
agreeable charms of music. By it we are enabled to enjoy the
pleasures of society, and reciprocally to communicate to each other
our thoughts and intentions, our purposes and desires; while thus
our reason is capable of exciting its utmost power and energy.
The wise and beneficent author of nature intended by the formation of this sense, that we should be social creatures, and receive
the greatest and most important part of our knowledge by the
information of others. For these purposes we are endowed with

Hearing that, by a proper exertion of our natural powers, our happiness may be complete." "Feeling is that sense by which we distinguish the different qualities of bodies; such as heat and cold, hardness and softness, roughness and smoothness, figure, solidity, motion, and extension." To a Mark Master Mason these two senses ever suggest that sacred tie which binds him to his brethren, and when he *hears* a brother's call for assistance he is taught that he should at once extend the *hand* of charity. In the eloquent language of Bro. A. T. C. PIERSON: "He that is deaf to the sufferings of a brother deserves no better fate than to be deprived of the great blessing of *hearing;* and he who is so callous to the wants of his brother as to refuse to stretch forth his hand to alleviate his sufferings deserves to have no hand to help himself."

And we will cut wood out of Lebanon, as much as thou shalt need; and will bring it to thee in floats by sea to Joppa, and thou shalt carry it up to Jerusalem.

The ancient city of Joppa, to which allusion is here made, is one of the oldest towns of Asia, and is situated on a rocky promontory jutting out from the eastern coast of the Mediterranean Sea, about forty miles in a northwesterly direction from Jerusalem. Its Greek name was Joppa, its Hebrew name Japho,* and it is now called Jaffa or Yaffa. It was, and still is, the principal seaport of the land of Judea, and of course a place of great commercial importance; but its harbor is bad, and ships generally anchor a mile from the town. From this port sailed the ships of the Israelitish kings,

* Joshua, xix. 46.

and to it came the treasures of Ethiopia and the riches of Ophir. It has now a mixed population of about five thousand. It is described by JOSEPHUS as a very dangerous haven on account of its bold precipitous shore, against which the north wind dashes immense waves.* Baron GERAMB, who visited the Holy Land, in 1842, has given a vivid description of the difficulty and danger attending a landing at this place, which has been partially quoted by Dr. MACKEY.†

Notwithstanding the difficulty and danger of the landing, and the subsequent ascent up the steep banks of the sea coast at that place, most of the materials for the temple were landed here, when they were brought down from Mount Lebanon. When the immense size and weight of these materials are considered, it seems almost incredible that they could have been conveyed to Jerusalem in that manner. But not only was this done at the building of the first temple, but we learn from Holy Scripture that the same was true of the second temple; for "They gave money also unto the masons, and to the carpenters; and meat, and drink, and oil, unto them of Zidon, and them of Tyre, to bring cedar trees from Lebanon to the sea of Joppa, according to the grant that they had of CYRUS, King of Persia."‡

*   *   *   *   *   *

Then he brought me back the way of the gate of the outward sanctuary, which looketh toward the East; and it was shut. And the LORD said unto me, Son of man, Mark Well, and behold with thine eyes, and hear with thine ears all that I say unto thee concerning all the ordinances of the house of the LORD, and all the laws thereof; and mark well the entering in of the house, with every going forth of the sanctuary.

* Josephus. Jewish Wars, B III. C. ix. S. ♂.
† Lexicon, p 232.   ‡ Ezra, iii. 7.

*   *   *   *   *   *

The Mark is the appropriate jewel of a Mark Master Mason.
The origin of the Mark is unknown. Perhaps the most reasonable
supposition is that it was adopted at a very early period as a
species of signature used by those who were unable to write.   The
traditions of the Order are to the effect that there were three
classes of Fellow-Crafts employed at the building of King SOLO-
MON's Temple.   One class wrought in the clayey grounds between
Succoth and Zeradatha, the second in the forests of Lebanon,
while the third or principal class was employed in the quarries of
Zarthan.   Those who wrought in the quarries were eighty thousand
in number, divided into Lodges of eighty each.   Over each of these
Lodges presided a Mark Master and two Mark Men as Wardens.
Each of these craftsmen was obliged to select a device which was
recorded in a scroll kept for that purpose, and, thereupon, became
the "Mark" of the brother, and could not be altered or changed.
A copy of this mark, the craftsman was required to put on all his
work, and thus every person's work could be readily distinguished,
and praise or censure be correctly bestowed without mistakes.   By
this wise precaution, such a vast body of men were easily and
correctly paid, and by its means the workmen were enabled to put
together with such facility and precision the materials when conveyed from the quarries to Mount Moriah.   The marks used by
our ancient brethren are said to have been invented by HIRAM
ABIFF, and consisted of combinations of the square, the level, the

plumb, and the cross. At a subsequent time, modifications of these marks were adopted by the Grand Masters as the Freemason's alphabet or cipher, which was used upon a memorable occasion.

The truth of these traditions is verified by the fact that such marks were in use by the operative Masons of the middle ages. STEINBRENNER, in describing the guilds of stonemasons of Germany, says that if the candidate's qualifications were deemed satisfactory, "he was at once taught the salute or '*gruss*' and the token or '*handschenk*' by which he could make himself known as a traveling Fellow-Craft. He also received a distinctive *mark*, which he was thenceforth obliged to place on all his work."*

Similar marks are to be found among all ancient ruins, and great numbers of them have been collected and described by M. DIDRON, a French writer, and also by G. GOODWIN, Esq., a member of the English Society of Antiquaries. Within a few years similar marks have been discovered in Mexico and Central America. From the similarity existing between them wherever found, it is conclusively shown that they must have been in general use by all builders at a very early period.

The primary use of the mark was undoubtedly that above mentioned, but they also very naturally came to be an equivalent in all transactions for the owner's name, and hence their use in the payment of wages. Hence, too, the "Mark" became the jewel of the Mark Master Mason, and was invested with the same properties as were attached to the Roman "*Tessera Hospitalis*," or hospitable token. When two persons in ancient times desired some emblem of their friendship, they selected a piece of bone, metal, or stone, and engraved upon it their names, their initials, or some device. This they divided into two pieces, each taking one. This was called a *Tessera Hospitalis*, and became the pledge of a friendship and attachment which nothing was permitted to destroy.

Though in itself considered of the smallest value, "yet as the memorial of a highly esteemed friend, it was retained and handed down from generation to generation, even to remote posterity; and whenever or wherever the two pieces were produced mutual assistance and protection were assured to the holders."

The "Mark" may be made of any durable material, and in any form, to suit the taste or fancy of the owner. On one side is generally engraved the owner's name, Chapter, and date of his

---

* Steinbrenner. Origin of Masonry p. 72.

advancement. On the other side must be engraved in a circular form these eight letters: H. T. W. S. S. T. K. S. Within this circle of letters is engraved the device selected by the brother, and when once chosen the whole should be drawn or recorded in a book kept for that purpose, and it is then said to be recorded in the "Lodge Book of Marks."

When this has been done the brother can neither alter nor change it, but it remains as his mark to the day of his death. Many Chapters fix by their laws the time within which each brother must select his mark, and where this is not the case, the general regulations of the degree make it the imperative duty of a brother to do so, as soon as possible, and within a reasonable time after his advancement.

The use of this jewel is thus beautifully explained by Dr. A. G. MACKEY: "This mark is not a mere ornamental appendage of the degree, but is a sacred token of the rites of friendship and brotherly love, and its presentation at any time by the owner to another Mark Master would claim from the latter certain acts of friendship which are of solemn obligation among the Fraternity. A mark thus presented for the purpose of obtaining a favor is said to be pledged; though remaining in the possession of the owner, it ceases for any actual purposes of advantage to be his property; Nor can it be again used by him until, either by the return of the favor, or the consent of the benefactor, it has been redeemed; for it is a positive law of the Order that no Mark Master shall pledge his mark a second time until he has redeemed it from its previous pledge." Should misfortunes assail the Mark Master Mason; should sickness fall upon him; should grim want come to his door, and gaunt hunger gnaw at his vitals; should the light of day be shut out from his sightless eyes, or his palsied tongue forget its office, his mark at once affords him immediate relief, and far surpasses in the magical pathos and power of its silent appeal, all the eloquence of studied language.

*   *   *   *   *   *

The traditions of the degree assert that the price of a mark is a "Bekah" or Jewish half shekel of silver, equal in value to the fourth part of a dollar. It has been claimed by some authors, that "the shekel was not a coin, but a definite weight of gold or silver

which, being weighed out, passed as current money among the Hebrews." This is undoubtedly a mistake.*

The selection of the "*Bekah*" or half shekel as the equivalent of a "mark" is probably in allusion to the "offering of the LORD" commanded to be made by the Israelites. "Every one that passeth among them that are numbered, from twenty years old and above, shall give an offering unto the LORD. The rich shall not give more, and the poor shall not give less than half a shekel, when they give an offering unto the LORD, to make an atonement for your souls. Exodus, xxx. 14, 15.

*   *   *   *   *   *

This is the stone which was set at naught of

---

* Union Bible Dictionary. The learned Dean Prideaux says: "There are many old Jewish shekels still in being, and others of the same sort are freyou builders, which is become the head of the corner.

*   *   *   *   *   *

This passage and the similar ones* which are introduced at an earlier period in the ceremonies, are quotations or paraphrases of the twenty-second verse of the 118th Psalm of DAVID, where the original language is used in reference to the promised Messiah. The design of the passage at this point is to teach us the great truth that nothing has been made in vain. It matters not how worthless and insignificant a creature may appear to our finite and prejudiced eyes, we should never despise it, nor cast it from us in derision, for we may rest assured that if Infinite Wisdom has been employed in its creation, it has in the economy of Providence its appropriate place and use. From it we may also learn never to despond or grow weary in well doing. Although our motives may be misinterpreted, and the work of our hands be misjudged by our erring fellow-men, still we may have faith that there is over all a JUDGE, who sees not with the eyes of man, and who will at the last make the stone which the builders rejected "the head of the corner."

The keystone is a striking symbol of the close union that should ever exist between brethren of the same household. As the operative Mason constructs his material arch so that the stones employed in its erection are made to depend for support on each other, and most of all on the keystone which binds them all together and completes the structure, so by this symbol we are taught that in the great arch of Freemasonry which spans the earth, we are dependant on each other for comfort and happiness, and most of all must rely for our social pleasures and blessings on that charity, which is the keystone to bind us together brother to brother, and which alone can render any society desirable.

*   *   *   *   *   *

quently dug up in Judea, with this inscription on them in Samaritan letters, Jerusalem Kedoshah, that is, Jerusalem the Holy; which inscription shows that they could not be the coin either of the Israelites of the ten tribes, or of the Samaritans who after succeeded them in their land; for neither of them would have put the name of Jerusalem upon their coin, or even have called it the holy city. These pieces, therefore, must have been the coin of those of the two tribes before the captivity." Connection, vol. 1, p. 449.

* Matt. xxi. 42.   Mark, xii. 10.   Luke, xx. 17.

The Working Tools of a Mark Master Mason are the Chisel and Mallet.

THE CHISEL

Is an instrument made use of by operative Masons to cut, carve, mark, and indent their work.   It morally demonstrates the advantages of discipline and education. The mind, like the diamond in its original state, is rude and unpolished; but as the effect of the chisel on the external coat soon presents to view the latent beauties of the diamond, so education discovers the latent virtues of the mind, and draws them forth to range the large field of matter and space, to display the summit of human knowledge, our duty to GOD and to man.

THE MALLET

Is an instrument made use of by operative Masons to knock off excrescences and smooth surfaces.   It morally teaches to correct irregularities, and reduce man to a proper level; so that by quiet deportment, he may, in the school of discipline, learn to be content.   What the mallet is to the workman enlightened reason is to the passions: it curbs ambition; it depresses envy; it moderates anger, and it encourages good dispositions; whence arises among good Masons that comely order,

> " Which nothing earthly gives, or can destroy,
> The soul's calm sunshine, and the heartfelt joy."

*   *   *   *   *   *

These symbolical explanations of the Chisel and Mallet were taken from the installation service of our English brethren in which they are included among the implements presented to the new Master.

The chisel was also formerly one of the working tools of an English Entered Apprentice, and as such was thus symbolized. "From the chisel we learn that perseverance is necessary to establish perfection; that the rude material receives its fine polish but from repeated efforts alone; that nothing short of indefatigable exertion can induce the habit of virtue, enlighten the mind, and render the soul pure."

*   *   *   *   *   *

The following passage of Scripture is also appropriately introduced and explained:

To him that overcometh will I give to eat of the hidden manna, and I will give him a white stone, and in the stone a new name written, which no man knoweth saving he that receiveth it.

*   *   *   *   *   *

The meaning of this and kindred passages from the Apocalypse has been the subject of much speculation. Dr. A. G. MACKEY, in a commentary on the above, says it is most probable that by the "white stone" and the "new name," St. JOHN referred to the *tesseræ hospitales* of the ancients.

Dr. OLIVER observes that "the white stone is an inestimable gift, promised to every one who lives a moral and virtuous life. White is an emblem of purity, and the new name conveys a title to be admitted within the vail, and honored with a seat near the living GOD, in that palace which is described by St. JOHN as a perfect cube, whose walls and foundations are garnished with all kinds of precious stones, all hewed, squared, and polished by the masterly hand of T. G. A. O. T. U."*

Some commentators have supposed the passage to allude to the practice among the ancients of passing judgment on an accused person. Those in favor of acquitting him cast a white ball into an urn, and those who adjudged him guilty cast in a black ball; a custom which has been perpetuated in one of the most important transactions of a Lodge.

If another opinion may be offered among so many, it would seem to be more probably an allusion to an ancient custom at the Olympian games, where white stones were given to the conquerors, with their names written upon them, and the value of the prize they had won. It is well known that many of the figures used by the New Testament writers were taken from these national games of Greece.† The symbolical teaching then intended to be conveyed to our minds is this: If we are victorious in our endeavors to reach the goal set before us, we shall receive for our reward, the white stone indicative of our purity of heart, and in it, the new name that shall be the passport for our admission into the Celestial Lodge above.

The new name may denote the adoption of the receiver into the family of GOD,‡ and hence the *white stone* may with propriety symbolize the adoption of the Mark Master Mason into a Fraternity whose only aim is to erect a spiritual temple to the GREAT I AM; and the *new name* will then become a symbol of that Great and Sacred Name, that Eternal Truth which leads the true Mason in search of light from his first step on the checkered pavement until he has passed the vails of the Tabernacle.

*   *   *   *   *   *

* Dr. Oliver's Dictionary of Masonry.

† Union Bible Dictionary, de Race.

‡ Isaiah. lxii. 2. Union Bible Dictionary.

CHARGE TO THE CANDIDATE

BROTHER: I congratulate you on having been thought worthy of being promoted to this honorable degree of Masonry. Permit me to impress it on your mind that your assiduity should ever be commensurate with your duties, which become more and more extensive as you advance in Masonry.

The situation to which you are now promoted will draw upon you not only the scrutinizing eyes of the world at large, but those also of your brethren, on whom this degree of Masonry has not been conferred; all will be justified in expecting your conduct and behavior to be such as may with safety be imitated.

In the honorable character of Mark Master Mason, it is more particularly your duty to endeavor to let your conduct in the world, as well as in the Lodge, and among your brethren, be such as may stand the test of the Grand Overseer's square, that you may not, like the unfinished and imperfect work of the negligent and unfaithful of former times, be rejected and thrown side, as unfit for that spiritual building, that house not made with hands, eternal in the heavens.

While such is your conduct, should misfortunes assail you, should friends forsake you, should envy traduce your good name, and malice persecute you; yet may you have confidence that, among Mark Master Masons, you will find friends who will administer relief to your distresses, and comfort your afflictions; ever bearing in mind, as a consolation under all the frowns of fortune, and as an encouragement to hope for better prospects, that *the stone which the builders rejected* (possessing merits to them unknown) *became the chief stone of the corner.*

The reader will observe that the authors of this work have restored the original charge as published by WEBB, and which was mutilated by JEREMY L. CROSS, and most of those who have followed him.

It will also be observed that this charge, unlike those of other degrees, is more properly a congratulatory address, and should always be given in that form.

*   *   *   *   *   *

The sixth hour of the sixth day of the week.

*   *   *   *   *   *

The last shall be first.

The following song may be sung:

Music—*America*

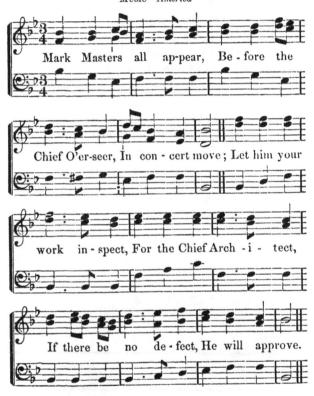

Mark Masters all ap-pear, Be - fore the Chief O'er-seer, In con - cert move; Let him your work in - spect, For the Chief Arch - i - tect, If there be no de - fect, He will approve.

You who have passed the square,
For your rewards prepare,
　　Join heart and hand;
Each with his mark in view.
March with the just and true;
Wages to you are due,
　　At your command.

HIRAM, the widow's son,
Sent unto SOLOMON
    Our great key-stone;
On it appears the name
Which raises high the fame
Of all to whom the same
    Is truly known.

Now to the westward move,
Where, full of strength and love,
    HIRAM doth stand;
But if impostors are
Mix'd with the worthy there,
Caution them to beware
    Of the right hand.

*   *   *   *   *   *

There are many traditions as to the amount of wages paid the workmen on the temple. One of these, which has been of late years somewhat extensively circulated in this country, is to the effect that those Fellow-Crafts who were "advanced to the honorary degree of a Mark Master Mason" were paid a Jewish shekel, or about fifty cents in the coin of the United States, for each day's labor.

Another tradition, current among our English brethren, relates that the men were paid in their Lodges by shekels, and the number of shekels per day was regulated by the square of the number of the degree which each order of men had attained. According to this theory, an Entered Apprentice received one shekel, or fifty cents; a Fellow-Craft, four, or two dollars; a Mark Man, nine, or four and one half dollars; a Mark Master, sixteen, or eight dollars, and in like manner until they make the highest grade to have received about forty dollars per day.

Both of these accounts are wholly fanciful, and were undoubtedly fabricated within the last fifty years, without the existence of any documents or authorities on which to base them. According to the ancient traditions and the early rituals, the true amount of wages paid a faithful craftsman who wrought in the quarries was a much smaller sum than those above named. The wages of a speculative craftsman is the knowledge of Divine Truth which the Grand Master of the Universe will bestow on him who faithfully performs his allotted labor in the quarries of earth.

The following parable is read:

It is like unto a man that is an householder, which went out early in the morning to hire laborers into his vineyard. And when he had agreed with the laborers for a penny a day, he sent them into his vineyard. And he went out about the third hour, and saw others standing idle in the market-place, and said unto them, Go ye also into the vineyard; and whatsoever is right I will give you. And they went their way. Again he went out about the sixth and ninth hour, and did likewise. And about the eleventh hour, he went out and found others standing idle, and saith unto them, Why stand ye here all the day idle? They say unto him, because no man hath hired us. He saith unto them, Go ye also into the vineyard; and whatsoever is right, that shall ye receive. So when even was come, the lord of the vineyard saith unto his steward, Call the laborers, and give them their hire, beginning from the last unto the first. And when they came that were hired about the eleventh hour, they received every man a penny. But when the first came, they supposed that they should have received more; and they likewise received every man a penny. And when they had received it, they murmured against the good man of the house, saying, These last have wrought but one hour, and thou hast made them equal unto us, which have borne the burden and heat of the day. But he answered one of them, and said, Friend, I do thee no wrong; didst not thou agree with me for a penny? Take that thine is, and go thy way; I will give unto this last even as unto thee. Is it not lawful for me to do what I will with mine own? Is thine eye evil because I am good? So the last shall be first, and the first last; for many be called, but few chosen.

*   *   *   *   *   *

The penny alluded to here was undoubtedly the Roman penny, a silver coin equal to from twelve and a half to fourteen cents in United States coin. A very erroneous impression prevails respecting the value of money in olden times, on account of our associations with its present value. A *penny*, equivalent to twelve or fourteen cents, seems to us to be a mean compensation for ten or twelve hours toil in the vineyard, and the *two pence* affords very equivocal evidence to our minds of generosity in the good Samaritan;* but, when it is considered how much of the comforts and necessaries of life these apparently trifling sums could obtain, the case appears differently. As lately as the year 1351 the price of labor was regulated in England by act of Parliament, and "hay-makers, corn-weeders, without meat, drink, or other courtesy" (in modern phrase, finding themselves), were to have a penny a day. In many places these were the highest wages paid for any kind of agricultural labor, some kinds being still less. The pay of a chaplain in England, in 1314, was three half pence, or about three cents a day. At the same time wheat was sixteen cents a bushel, and a fat sheep only twelve cents. A penny a day under such circumstances would not be inconsiderable wages. In the fourth century before CHRIST a penny would have bought, it is estimated, at least ten times more than it would have done in England in the year 1780—and prices then were very much lower than at the present day.*

The use of this parable, and also the quotations from the New Testament, are said to be "*Americanisms*"—although this may be safely doubted. It is true, the parable does not form a part of the ritual of the degree of "*Master Mark Mason*," as found among the detached degrees of the Ancient and Accepted rite; but this is not by any means conclusive that it was added by the early American ritualists. At all events these anachronisms have become of such

* Luke, x., 35.   † Union Bible Dictionary.

long standing that they cannot now be discarded even were such a thing desirable.

The great moral lessons taught us in this degree are concisely and eloquently enforced by the symbolism of this sublime parable. As a Fellow-Craft we are taught that "the internal and not the external qualifications of a man are what Masonry regards."* As a Mark Master Mason we learn the great truth that the Eternal Father is no respecter of persons, but will bestow the gifts of his beneficent hand alike to each one who sincerely labors to obey his righteous law.

"The design of all Masonry is the search after Truth, and every one who seeks to discover it shall receive his reward in the attainment of it." So in the vineyard of Masonry it matters not whether we commenced our labors with the rising sun, and have borne the burden and heat of the day, or whether we came in at the eleventh hour, just as the day was drawing to a close, if we but do our duty, if we are faithful and earnest, we shall receive our wages in a clear conscience, and in the commendation "well done good and faithful servant."

*   *   *   *

Now to the praise of those
Who triumphed o'er the foes
    Of Mason's art;
To the praiseworthy three,
Who founded this degree;
May all their virtues be
    Deep in our hearts.

The ceremonies previous to closing a Lodge in this degree are peculiarly interesting. They teach us the duty we owe to our brethren in particular, and the whole family of mankind in general, by ascribing praise to the meritorious, and dispensing rewards to the diligent and industrious.

* Charge in second degree.

PAST MASTER

THIS degree is more closely associated with Symbolic than Chapter Masonry. It was originally, and is to this day, an honorary degree, and should be conferred only on the newly-elected Master of a Lodge. But as it has become a permanent component part of the Capitular system, it is, therefore, useless to contend with what is often termed the "inconsistency" of conferring an honor where no equivalent services have been, or are expected to be, rendered.

As the rulers of Masonry are, and should only be, selected for their superior skill and intelligence, they alone should be permitted to receive the valuable light and information contained in the ceremonies of this degree.

Those who receive the degree in the Chapter are termed "virtual" Past Masters, in contradistinction to those who have been elected and installed in a regularly constituted Symbolic Lodge, who are called "actual" Past Masters; the former having no rights or privileges, as such, out of the Chapter.

In order to harmonize many of the controversies that were constantly arising in respect to the contending rights of Past Masters, the General Grand Chapter of the United States, in 1856, adopted a resolution recommending the Chapters under its jurisdiction "to abridge the ceremonies now conferred in the Past Master's degree within the narrowest constitutional limits, only retaining the inducting of the candidate into the Oriental Chair, and communicating the means of recognition."

The various sections of the lecture of this degree, which relate to the constitution and dedication of new Lodges; the installation of officers; the laying of cornerstones; the dedication of Masonic halls, and the funeral services, being only necessary to the actual Past Masters, are to be found in connection with the Symbolic degrees, under the title of "Ancient Ceremonies."

HISTORY

WHEN the Order of Past Master was first made a constituent part of the service used at the installation of a Master of a Lodge, or whence the ceremonies of that Order were derived, are problems that have never yet been solved, although the Past Master's degree has been more discussed than all the other grades of Freemasonry.

The earliest allusions to the Order of Past Master are those which are found in DERMOTT's Ahiman Rezon, and PRESTON's Illustrations, where it is spoken of as a long-established thing, whose possession by a Master could not be dispensed with, and the conferring of which was the only esoteric portion of the ceremonies of installation. That it was in use among both the *Ancients* and *Moderns* is, therefore, certain, and, by both, was recognized as being of ancient and binding obligation.

The reader will bear in mind that at the organization of the Royal Arch degree as a separate and distinct grade, it could only be conferred on Masters of Lodges.

This was one of the fundamental Landmarks of the original Royal Arch system. At first it was well enough; but in later years, when the Fraternity became more extended, this ancient regulation so limited the number of Royal Arch Masons that the excellent precepts of Capitular Masonry lost much of their effect by reason of the want of numbers sufficiently interested and duly qualified to teach them. It, therefore, became necessary to give up the general practice of the entire system or relax the above mentioned rule. So binding was the Landmark considered that, rather than violate it, the fathers of Royal Arch Masonry contrived the ceremony of "privately passing the chair." This was nothing more nor less than the creation of a *Virtual* in place of an *Actual* Master, and was done by virtue of a dispensation from the Grand Master. The candidate, after receiving this degree of Past Master was considered as eligible to the Royal Arch as if he were an Actual Past Master, and the Landmark was still preserved. In England, however, since the union in 1813, the ancient Landmark has been abrogated, and the candidate for exaltation is required to possess neither the Order nor the degree of Past Master.

In Ireland, Scotland, and the United States, the ancient Landmark is still preserved, and in the latter country the rights, duties, and privileges of both Actual and Virtual Past Masters have been thoroughly discussed, and are now generally well understood.

It is now settled that the Order of Past Master is a part of the necessary installation service to be conferred upon a Master elect of a Lodge, and that a Master cannot be lawfully installed without receiving that Order; that Chapter Past Masters cannot confer the Order of Past Master upon a Master elect, nor be present when it is conferred; that an Actual Past Master cannot sit in a Lodge of Virtual Past Masters; and that a Virtual Past Master can claim no right, privilege, or immunity in a Lodge or among Actual Past Masters, by virtue of his having received the degree of Past Master.

In short the degree of Past Master is conferred in the Capitular system for Chapter purposes only; "and entitles none who receive it to the honors accorded to one who has regularly passed the chair of a subordinate Lodge."

The degree was not regularly introduced into the American system or rite until somewhere about the year 1792. Previous to that time it was the custom, generally, to convene the necessary number who had received it, and by dispensation of the Grand Master, confer the degree on candidates in an occasional Lodge, which acted for the time being, by virtue of the dispensation.*

The degree was also formerly conferred by the Lodges of Perfection under the Ancient and Accepted rite. The same regulation existed there, as in the Royal Arch, that none but Past Masters should be eligible for the degrees, and, therefore, whenever a candidate, who was not an Actual Past Master, presented himself, the degree of Past Master was in the first place conferred upon him. I have now before me the records of a Lodge of Perfection, bearing date 1782, in which the above facts appear. After the Chapters began to assume jurisdiction over the degree, the councils of the Ancient and Accepted rite relinquished their claim to it, and its status after much discussion is now well understood, and the degree itself is much better appreciated than formerly.

* The degree is now conferred in a similar manner in the jurisdiction of Pennsylvania, which has never come under the General Grand Chapter.

OFFICERS

THE regular officers of a Past Master's Lodge are:

1. RIGHT WORSHIPFUL MASTER;
2. SENIOR GRAND WARDEN;
3. JUNIOR GRAND WARDEN.

The officers of a Chapter take rank in a Past Master's Lodge as follows, viz: the High-Priest as R. W. Master; the King as Senior Grand Warden; the Scribe as Junior Grand Warden; the Treasurer and Secretary occupy the corresponding stations; the Principal Sojourner as Senior Deacon; the Royal Arch Captain as Junior Deacon, and the Tiler at his proper station.

The symbolic color of the Past Master's degree is purple. The apron is of white lambskin, square at the corners, edged with purple, and the jewel of the degree inscribed upon it. The collar is purple, edged with gold.

 The jewel of a Past Master is a pair of compasses, extended to sixty degrees, the points resting on the segment of a circle. Between the extended legs of the compasses is a flaming sun. The whole may be suspended within a circle.

Lodges of Past Masters are "dedicated to the Holy Saint JOHN."

The candidate receiving this degree is said to be "inducted into the Oriental Chair of King SOLOMON."

OPENING

THE following may be used as a charge at opening a Lodge in this degree:

Blessed is the man that walketh not in the counsel of the ungodly, nor standeth in the way of sinners, nor sitteth in the seat of the scornful: But his delight is in the law of the LORD; and in his law doth he meditate day and night. And he shall be like a tree planted by the rivers of water, that bringeth forth his fruit in his season; his leaf also shall not wither; and whatsoever he doeth shall prosper. The ungodly are not so; but are like the chaff which the wind driveth away. Therefore, the ungodly shall not stand in the judgment, or sinners in the congregation of the righteous. For the LORD knoweth the way of the righteous; but the way of the ungodly shall perish.

*   *   *   *   *   *

RITUAL

SECTION FIRST

THIS section treats of the government of our society; the disposition of our rulers; and their requisite qualifications. It also illustrates the ceremonies of conferring this distinguished honor upon such as are found worthy.

* * * * * *

RECEPTION

* * * * * *

PREVIOUS to the investiture of the candidate, he is reminded of the responsibilities he is about to assume, and his obligations to the Fraternity are enforced in the way peculiar to the Craft.

* * * * * *

THE GIBLEMITES

IN a recent work by Past Grand Master A. T. C. PIERSON, there are collected many traditions which have been current at different periods among the Fraternity. Many of them are fanciful and without any known warrant of authority, being generally of English origin. Among this last class is the following: "During the process of the erection of the temple, SOLOMON was in the habit of visiting every part of the building, to inspect the work and examine the progress being made. Upon one occasion, as he was ascending a ladder of rope, one side gave way, but just as he was falling, he was caught by two of the workmen who happened to be passing, and he was thus saved from great injury if not from death. These workmen were Giblemites, and in gratitude to them for the service rendered him, and to perpetuate its remembrance, SOLOMON took this class under his especial protection, and ordered that in the future he should be constantly attended by two of the

Giblemites. When age, infirmity, and disease had rendered SOLOMON unable to walk alone, two of this favored class constantly attended and assisted him even to seating him upon his throne."[*] Although much of this tradition is entirely without authority to sustain it, yet there is in it some truth; and we may derive from it the important lesson, one which we may see constantly verified around us, that even the wisest, best, and most exalted of men are at all times dependent on the charity of their fellows, and the bounty of Divine Providence.

The Giblemites were the people of Gebal, a city of Phœnicia, north of Beyroot, called Byblos by the Greeks and Romans, now known by the name of *Jiblah.* At the present time it is but little more than a mass of ruins, which are sufficiently magnificent to indicate its former greatness and beauty. Indeed it was famous in former times for the skill of its masons and builders, who excelled all others in the knowledge of architecture. We find them frequently mentioned in Scripture as "stone squarers," a term applied to them as being eminently distinguished in that kind of work.

*   *   *   *   *   *

The candidate is then regularly invested with the insignia of office, and the furniture and implements of the Lodge are presented and explained.

The Master's jewel is a square, and inculcates morality. It was a saying of ARISTOTLE that "he who bears the shocks of fortune valiantly, and demeans himself uprightly, is truly good, and of a square posture, without reproof." The Master should, therefore, never lose sight of the important lesson which his jewel symbolically teaches, but on every occasion, and by all his acts, prove that he is in truth, a square stone in the temple of Masonry.

The *Holy Writings*, that great light in Masonry, will guide you to all truth; it will direct your paths to the temple of happiness, and point out to you the whole duty of man.

* Traditions of Freemasonry, p. 294.

The *Square* teaches us to regulate our actions by rule and line, and to harmonize our conduct by the principles of morality and virtue.

The *Compass* teaches to limit our desires in every station, that, rising to eminence by merit, we may live respected and die regretted.

The *Rule* directs that we should punctually observe our duty, press forward in the path of virtue, and, neither inclining to the right nor to the left, in all our actions have eternity in view.

The *Line* teaches the criterion of moral rectitude, to avoid dissimulation in conversation and action, and to direct our steps to the path which leads to immortality.

You now receive in charge the *Charter* or *Warrant*, by the authority of which this Lodge is held. You are carefully to preserve it, and in no case should it ever be out of your immediate control, and duly transmit it to your successor in office.

The *Book of Constitutions* you are to search at all times. Cause it to be read in your Lodge, that none may pretend ignorance of the excellent precepts it enjoins.

You will also receive in charge the *By-Laws* of your Lodge, which you are to see carefully and punctually executed.

You will also receive in charge the Records of the Lodge, which you are to see correctly kept, that nothing improper is committed to paper; and for this reason you are to have a general supervision over the duties of the Secretary.

*   *   *   *   *   *

*   *   *   *   *   *

The following song may be introduced, accompanied with the *honors:*

PAST MASTER'S ODE

Air—*Peterboro'*

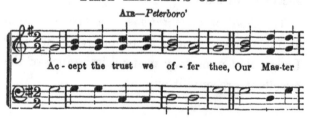

Ac - cept the trust we of - fer thee, Our Mas-ter

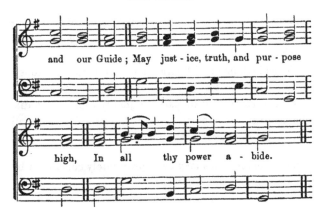

and our Guide; May just-ice, truth, and pur-pose

high, In all thy power a - bide.

GOD help, in thy extended charge,
    To keep our temple fair;
To rear it higher, higher still,
    The temple of thy care.

Oh! lead us by the light of truth,
    To walk in wisdom's way,
Through all the trying paths of life,
    To realms of endless day.

❡

* * * The duties appertaining to the Chair are
many and various. They consist in opening, instructing,
and closing Lodges; initiating, crafting, and raising
Masons; presiding at funeral obsequies and all other
duties connected therewith.

*   *   *   *   *   *

The duties appertaining to the Chair are recounted

and explained, and the necessary assistants in their discharge are selected, according to the ancient Landmarks.

These lessons are illustrated by ceremonies, through which every Master of a Lodge, from time immemorial, has been compelled to pass, to qualify him for the discharge of those important duties that devolve upon all who wield the gavel in the East.

These ceremonies may be appropriately concluded by the delivery of the following

CHARGE TO THE CANDIDATE

MY BROTHER: The Past Master's degree, unlike all the other degrees of Freemasonry, sheds no light upon itself. It was formerly conferred only on Masters of Lodges, to instruct them in the duties they owed the Lodges over which they were called to preside, and likewise the duties of the brethren to the Chair; but we, as Royal Arch Masons, confer this degree, not only as a preliminary step, but also for the more important purpose of guarding us against a breach of our Masonic obligations. We are all, my brother, too apt to come forward and kneel at our sacred altar and take upon ourselves the most solemn obligations to perform certain duties, and then behave as if we had not done so. This, my brother, is not as it should be.

Let the scene which you have this evening witnessed be a striking lesson to you, and not only to you, but to us all as Masons, never to lose sight of the solemn obligations which we have all taken upon ourselves of our own free will, and in the most solemn manner promised that we would never violate.

It becomes your duty as a Past Master, by amiable, discreet, and virtuous conduct, to convince mankind of the goodness of the institution; so that when a person is said to be a member of it, the world may know that he is one to whom the burdened heart may pour out its sorrows; to whom distress may prefer its suit; whose hand is guided by justice, and whose heart is expanded by benevolence.

If you have any doubt of the extent of your obligations, a daily recourse to the Scriptures of Divine Truth will set you right. It will make your duties plain, and the discharge of them a pleasure rather than a burden. Make then the Holy Bible, that Great Light in Masonry, the man of your counsels, and the meditation of your heart.

It will never mislead nor deceive you, but a strict observance of its holy precepts will fit and prepare you for usefulness in this life, and for a glorious inheritance in that which is to come.

———•———

CLOSING

*   *   *   *   *   *

THE following invocation is appropriate to be used in closing a Lodge of Past Masters:

Help us, O GOD of our salvation, for the glory of thy Name, and deliver us, and purge away our sins, for thy Name's sake.

MOST EXCELLENT MASTER

This degree has special reference to that important period when the temple erected by King Solomon for the worship of Jehovah was completed and consecrated in all its glory and beauty.

None but those who, through diligence and industry, have progressed far toward perfection; none but those who have been seated in the Oriental Chair by the unanimous suffrages of their brethren, can be admitted to this degree.

In its original establishment, when the Temple of Jerusalem was finished, and the Fraternity celebrated the cape-stone with great joy, it is demonstrable that none but those who had proved themselves to be complete masters of their profession were admitted to this honor; and, indeed, the duties incumbent on every Mason, who is "received and acknowledged" as a Most Excellent Master, are such as render it indispensable that he should have a perfect knowledge of all the preceding degrees.

It was, therefore, a part of the wisdom and justice of SOLOMON'S plan to bestow upon many of his most skillful workmen some distinguishing mark of his approval. No higher appreciation of valuable services could have been rendered to the worthy and meritorious than conferring upon them an Order of Merit, with the honorable title of "Most Excellent Master." And it is still retained by us as a memorial of the method adopted by the King of Israel to distinguish the most skillful portion of the Craft, and to reward them for their services in behalf of the Fraternity.

HISTORY

THERE are several degrees bearing the name of Excellent, which have been practiced in different countries; but none of those now in use have any resemblance to the Most Excellent Master's degree of the American rite. The Excellent of Ireland has reference to the legation of MOSES; the Excellent of Scotland is very similar to what is known by passing the vails, alluding to a preparatory ceremony among the Hebrew captives at Babylon previous to their departure to rebuild the Temple at Jerusalem. The Super Excellent likewise differs in every country from the Most Excellent degree.

The latter has been considered by some recent writers as purely an American invention. It has been asserted that it was manufactured at Providence, Rhode Island, at the very close of the last century, an opinion, however, which cannot be sustained. Others have supposed it to have been arranged by the Rev. JONATHAN NYE and the Rev. GEORGE RICHARDS, two eminent Masons of the last century; but no substantial proof of this allegation has ever been adduced. A third origin has been assigned to the degree, which is that it was manufactured from fragmentary traditions by THOMAS SMITH WEBB. The main reason for this belief seems to be the fact that WEBB first gave an account of it in his *Freemason's Monitor*, published in 1797. It is quite probable that he may have rearranged the degree, or rather that he was one of the parties who arranged it in connection with the other degrees previous to his publication of the monitorial parts of it; but I have good reason to affirm that he could not have been the inventor of the degree. The late venerable Bro. WADSWORTH, of New York, has stated, without doubt correctly, the fact that WEBB did not acquire the Prestonian Lectures until 1795, an opinion corroborated by the investigations of Bro. ROB. MORRIS, and all those who have examined the origin of what is known as the WEBB Lectures.

It is, however, a well-known fact that the degree existed substantially as now worked, at least two or three years prior to that time, and hence it is perfectly apparent that WEBB did not originate the degree, however he may have improved its ritual.

The truth about the matter is probably this, that the degree was one of those supplementary or detached degrees which arose during the eighteenth century, and, in the chaotic state of Masonry in this country about 1790, was incorporated into the regular Capitular system to supply a hiatus in the rituals which has been lamented by intelligent craftsmen of other countries, but which has never been satisfactorily supplied except in the American rite. The third degree left the temple unfinished, and the Royal Arch noted its destruction. Its completion and solemn consecration; its gorgeous ceremonial and worship; its use as the central glory of the Jewish nation for four hundred years are passed over in perfect silence by the rituals of all other rites; to the American rite alone must the Masonic student turn if he would understand the full import of the complete allegory of Freemasonry.

OFFICERS

THE regular Officers of a Most Excellent Master's Lodge are:

1. RIGHT WORSHIPFUL MASTER;
2. SENIOR GRAND WARDEN.

Some writers add:

3. JUNIOR GRAND WARDEN,

on the supposition that ADONIRAM filled that office at the dedication of the temple, a theory entirely at variance with the old rituals, which make that office to have been vacant for a reason well known to the Craft. The officers of a Chapter take rank as follows, viz: The High-Priest as R. W. Master; the King as S. G. Warden, and, for the purposes of reception, the Principal Sojourner acts as Senior Deacon; the Royal Arch Captain as Junior Deacon, the Captain of the Host as Marshal, and the Treasurer, Secretary, and Tiler, fill their respective stations.

The symbolic color of the Most Excellent Master's degree is purple. The apron is of white lambskin, edged with purple, and the collar of purple edged with gold.

A candidate receiving this degree is said to be "received and acknowledged as a Most Excellent Master." Lodges of Most Excellent Masters are dedicated to K. S.

OPENING

*   *   *   *   *   *

THE following passage of Scripture is read at

OPENING

The earth is the LORD'S, and the fullness
thereof; the world, and they that dwell therein.
For he hath founded it upon the seas, and
established it upon the floods. Who shall
ascend into the hill of the LORD? and who
shall stand in his holy place? He that hath
clean hands and a pure heart; who hath not
lifted up his soul unto vanity, nor sworn
deceitfully. He shall receive the blessing from
the LORD, and righteousness from the GOD of
his salvation. This is the generation of them
that seek him, that seek thy face, O JACOB.
Selah. Lift up your heads, O ye gates, and be
ye lift up, ye everlasting doors; and the King
of Glory shall come in. Who is this King of
Glory? The LORD strong and mighty, the LORD
mighty in battle. Lift up your heads, O ye

gates; even lift them up, ye everlasting doors;
and the King of Glory shall come in.   Who is
the King of Glory ?   The LORD of hosts, he is
the King of Glory.

*   *   *   *   *   *

This Psalm is generally thought by commentators to have been
composed by DAVID upon the solemn occasion of bringing the Ark
of GOD from the house of OBED-EDOM into the Tabernacle which
had been built for it.   The Ark of GOD is supposed to be moving
in a grand and solemn procession of the whole Israelitish nation,
toward the place of its residence on Mount Zion.   On ascending the
mount, the Psalm is chanted in the rich and swelling notes of the
Hebrew music.   The celebrated commentator MATTHEW POOLE*
says that this was probably the purpose for which this Psalm was
written, but adds, "that DAVID had a further prospect, even to the
temple which he ardently desired to build, and which he knew
would be built by SOLOMON, and when that was done, and the Ark
was brought into it, then this Psalm was to be sung."   He adds,
that DAVID's Psalms were not only used by him upon the first
occasion for which he made them, but they also had a reference
prophetically to future events.

What could be more appropriate to the opening ceremonies of
this degree than this sublime Psalm chanted upon two occasions
by the Jews, when removing the Ark of the Covenant into the
places solemnly prepared for its reception.

*Annotations of the Holy Bible.   Folio edition, Glasgow, 1762.

RITUAL

♫ ♫ ♫

* * * * * *

THE Most Excellent Master's degree is designed to commemorate the completion and dedication of the temple. Nothing could be more appropriate, therefore, than setting up at the very entrance of the degree that keystone which, rejected of the builders, was destined to bind together the principal arch, and complete the temple. When the labor was brought to a successful close, and this degree was established, a new tie was created between the faithful craftsmen, and so in like manner we may learn the important lesson that the tenets of our Institution should bind and cement us together in the bonds of speculative Masonry, one common brotherhood.

* * * * * *

The following Psalm is read during the ceremony of

RECEPTION:

♩

I was glad when they said unto me, Let us go into the house of the LORD.

♫

Our feet shall stand within thy gates, O Jerusalem. Jerusalem is builded as a city that is compact together:

♫ ♩

Whither the tribes go up, the tribes of the LORD, unto the testimony of ISRAEL, to give thanks unto the name of the LORD.

♫ ♫

For there are set thrones of judgment, the thrones of the house of DAVID.

♫ ♫ ♩

Pray for the peace of Jerusalem: they shall prosper that love thee. Peace be within thy walls, and prosperity within thy palaces.

♫ ♫ ♫

For my brethren and companions' sakes, I will now say, Peace be within thee. Because of the house of the LORD our GOD I will seek thy good.

This Psalm was written by DAVID for the use of the people, when they came up to Jerusalem, to the solemn feasts, unto the "testimony;" that is, up to the Ark of the Covenant which was in Jerusalem. Three times in each year the devout Jews went up to Jerusalem, to acknowledge the mercies and give thanks unto the name of JEHOVAH ; and with great joy did they keep these returning festivals of their religion. How appropriate the words of this glorious Psalm ! How the heart thrills with emotion, as we go up to the dedication of our mystic temple, to the stirring strains of DAVID's harp ! And how touchingly we are reminded that we are not only to dedicate our earthly temple to Jehovah, but also our spiritual building—and how all these solemn ceremonies impress our hearts with the desire to exclaim, "Let us go into the House of the Lord not made with hands, eternal in the heavens."

* * * * * *

* * * * * *

A Most Excellent Master

The Holy Scriptures, as well as the traditions of the Fraternity, relate "that DAVID gave to SOLOMON the pattern of all that he had by the spirit," for the construction of the temple, and all its varied furniture and fixtures. It is also related traditionally that King Solomon, having completed every part of the work according to this pattern, resolved to reward the best informed and most skillful of the Giblemites, by creating them Most Excellent Masters. The traditions of the Craft contain much information relative to the privileges and duties of those who were admitted to this high rank. None were received but those who had proved themselves complete masters of their profession, or, as we would now say, had served as Masters of Lodges. The labor on the temple was finished, and many of the Craftsmen were soon to leave Judea in search of employment elsewhere. They had labored long, and with unexampled fidelity and zeal, encouraged and sustained by the hope that they should become Master Masons at the completion of the temple. Providence, in a sudden and mysterious manner, had prevented a full consummation of this hope, though they had been permitted to receive the shadow in lieu of the substance; and now King Solomon resolved still further to reward their fidelity. They were therefore set apart as teachers and masters of the art, and, as such, were charged to dispense Masonic light and knowledge among the uninformed and ignorant. In this character they were to travel into foreign countries, and carry into those lands that same sublime knowledge of Masonry which had, under the inspired wisdom of Solomon, wrought out from the quarry and the forest the wondrous beauties of Jerusalem's pride and glory.

This tradition is confirmed by the derivation of the title conferred on them. The Jews had three titles of respect which they gave to their doctors and teachers : Rab, Rabbi, and Rabban or Rabboni. Our title, Most Excellent Master, is equivalent to the designation Rabboni, which was the highest title of honor known to the Jews, and one that implies the possession of the highest rank and learning.

THE DEDICATION OF THE TEMPLE

Dedication is defined to be a religious ceremony by which any person, place or thing is set apart for the service of God or to some sacred use. The Altar,* the vessels of Joram,† the Tabernacle of Moses,‡ and the Temple of Solomon, were all dedicated to the service of God. The practice of consecration was very common among the Jews, and was suited to the peculiar dispensation under which they lived. Cities, walls, gates and even private dwellings were consecrated by peculiar ceremonies. The custom was preserved so long as the Jews had a country of their own, and is still retained, in modern times, in the consecration of churches and chapels. It is also practiced among Freemasons in the dedication of their halls and the consecration of their Lodges.

When the temple was nearly completed, a circumstance occurred which threw a sudden gloom over the Craft, and, for a time, dispelled the pleasures derived from the anticipation of a speedy and successful conclusion of their labors.

By that event the final completion and dedication of the magnificent edifice were delayed for several months. At length, however, King Solomon set apart a day for those solemn ceremonies, and caused proclamation to be made throughout all Israel, that all the Priests, Levites and people should gather themselves together for the purpose of celebrating the completion of the temple, and bringing up the Ark of the Covenant.

It is stated in the Scriptural account,§ that the dedication ceremonies lasted seven days, which were followed by the Feast of Tabernacles, which also lasted seven days from the evening of the 15th of Tisri, to the evening of the 22d day of the same month. The day of holy convocation was the 23d day of Tisri, on which the people were dismissed to their homes. The dedication ceremonies must have commenced on the evening of the 8th day of Tisri, the seventh month of the year 3001, and on the 9th the Ark was brought up and placed in the temple. The next day, or the 10th day of Tisri, was the Day of Atonement, the most sacred and solemn of the Jewish festivals, when the High-Priest, for the first time, went into the Sanctum Sanctorum of the Temple, before the Mercy Seat, to make atonement for the people of Israel. It is therefore quite evident that the temple could not have been dedicated on the 23d of Tisri, as has been stated by some authors.

The scriptural account is very concise, and contains no allusion to any ceremony like that of placing the copestone; but as the

* Numbers, viii. 84.   † 2 Samuel, viii. 11.   ‡ Exodus, xl.

§ Compare 1 Kings, viii. with 2 Chronicles, vii. 8.

completion of public edifices is now, and always has been, signalized by some ceremony, it is natural to suppose that such an important event as the completion of the temple would not have been allowed to pass without something being done to mark the event.

Our Masonic traditions, in accordance with this natural supposition, relate that the cope-stone or key-stone was brought forth, and, amidst the plaudits of the workmen and assembled people, was placed in the principal arch by the Grand Master himself.

Placing the Key-stone in the Principal Arch

Modern Masonic writers have indulged in much speculation as to what particular stone was used in the grand and imposing celebration of the completion of the temple. This difference of opinion as to the precise stone has led to a corresponding disagreement among the rituals of the degree in use among the Fraternity.*

---

* Dr. Oliver, in writing of this subject, observes that the word *key-stone* was originally and correctly used, although, to quote his language, "The Supreme Grand Chapter has substituted the words *cape-stone*, under an impression, we suppose, that arches and key-stones were unknown at the building of Solomon's Temple. But subsequent investigations have shown the inaccuracy of this opinion. It is now clear that the arch and key-stone were known to the Tyrians before the time of Solomon." *Origin of the English Royal Arch*, p. 23. This, by the way, is another instance of the innovations made by our English companions in the ritual of Freemasonry. It furnishes another striking proof of

The difficulty of attempting a satisfactory explanation does not consist in there being any error or inconsistency in the correct ritual of the degree, but simply in the necessity of using only such terms as do not contravene the established rules of the Order. It will be evident to any one who will examine the subject that the words "*cape-stone*," "*cope-stone*," "*cap-stone*," "*chief-stone*," and "*key-stone*," were formerly used as synonymous and convertible terms, and as such were applied to one and the same stone.* It is impossible to make extended quotations, but the following will suffice to show the fact, which may be verified to any extent from the early writers:

ANDERSON says "the *cape-stone* was celebrated with great joy."†

WEBB says "The Fraternity celebrated the *cape-stone* with great joy."‡

In the Most Excellent Master's song, written by WEBB, the following expressions are used, all evidently alluding to the same stone: "The cape-stone is finished;"§ "The key-stone to lay;"‖ "To bring forth the cape-stone with shouting and praise."‖

Dr. WORCESTER defines "*cope*" as "Anything spread over the head, as the concave of the sky, *the arch work over a door*."

WEBSTER's Dictionary, edition of 1864, defines "*cope*" as "Anything regarded as extended over the head, as the arch or concave of the sky, the roof or covering of a house, *the arch over a door, etc.*"

The stone used in the older and correct American rituals is the "*key-stone*," that identical stone "which the builders threw away."¶

the superior knowledge possessed by the early American Masons relative to the temple and the Jewish nation. It also demonstrates that the innovation of introducing the word "*cape-stone*," or "*cope-stone*" *in the sense of the top-most stone of the building,* is not chargeable to those "who constructed the American system," as has been alleged, but to the Supreme Grand Chapter of England.

* The word "*cape-stone*" is not to be found in any Lexicon within my reach, and was used by the early authors either ignorantly for "*cope-stone*," or intentionally, as some have supposed, to coin a word that should have a technical Masonic meaning. Dr. Mackey has the following language: "The cape-stone, or, as it would more correctly be called, the *cope-stone*," evidently considering that the former word was originally used for the latter.

† Constitutions. Edition 1783, p. 14.

‡ Webb's Monitor. Introduction to the Most Excellent Master's degree.

§ Verse 1.   ‖ Verse 2.

¶ A recent writer, who is much attached to the English system, asserts, however, that confounding this stone with the key-stone of the Mark degree is a prominent error. The same misconception as to the true stone used in this

For the want of it, the Craft were at a stand; upon it depended nothing less than the completion of the temple; it was found and applied to its intended use; "it bound together the *principal arch* and completed King SOLOMON'S Temple."

This "*principal arch* has been understood by the ablest ritualists and scholars, to have been the arch over the partition between the "holy place" and the "most holy place," the *principal entrance* as it has been called. The *Sanctum Sanctorum* was, as its name imports, the most sacred part of the temple; the oracle; the very essence, as it were, of the whole structure; the principal thing to which the rest of the building was only an auxiliary. Hence the arch over the entrance to this most sacred place is very properly denominated the principal arch of the temple.

The traditions relate that the stone was put in its place under the immediate supervision of the Grand Master himself in the presence of the priests and chief men who had entered the "holy place," and that thus the last act in the completion of the magnificent edifice was performed on the dedication morning by the self-same hands that leveled the foundation-stone more than eight years before. To suppose, therefore, that the stone used in this degree is the same stone found at a subsequent period is at variance with the ritual and traditions of the Order, and utterly inconsistent with the plainest dictates of common sense. The key-stone which completed the principal arch was laid by King SOLOMON in the presence of the Most Excellent Masters; while that stone which was discovered centuries after must have been placed in its position in secrecy, because its very existence and location was unknown to all the workmen at the temple, except a very limited number. Besides, this latter stone was placed in its position, months before the dedication, inasmuch as that part of the temple was completed, and certain articles deposited therein, before the Pillar of Beauty was broken. The last deposit was also made

degree has led the same author to remark that "one of the errors in this degree is the combining of the two celebrations, the celebration of the placing of the cope-stone, and the dedication of the temple in one and the same ceremony without explanation or intermission." On the other hand Dr. Mackey favors the opinion that the key-stone was appropriately used in this degree, but with strange inconsistency adds "that it was deposited on the day of the completion in the place for which it was intended, all of which relates to a mystery not unfolded in this degree"—thus evidently alluding to a still different key-stone; one which could not have been placed in its position in public amid the plaudits of the people.

before the dedication, and the sepulcher of the Omnific Symbol was then forever closed. Again the stone subsequently found* was among the foundations of the temple, while on the other hand the whole theory of the ritual is that the stone used in the commemoration of the final completion of the temple was placed in a higher locality. As we have seen, that locality was in the "*cope,*" or the arch over the entrance to the "Holy of Holies" or principal arch of the temple.

Bringing forth the Ark of the Covenant with shouting and praise.

The tabernacle of MOSES and the altar of burnt offering were left in the high place of Gibeon; but DAVID prepared a tent or tabernacle for the Ark of the Covenant in the city of DAVID, on Mount Zion. Sacred history informs us that DAVID, and the elders, and the captains of thousands, and all Israel, brought up from the house of Obed-Edom the Ark of the Covenant of the

* This latter stone was undoubtedly wrought by the same celebrated artist that fashioned the one mentioned in the Mark degree and again in this degree, for the reason that both of them bore the same mark.

LORD, with shouting and with sound of the cornet, and with
trumpets, and with cymbals, making a noise with psalteries and
harps, and set it in the midst of the tent that DAVID had pitched
for it.   There it remained until the dedication of the temple, when
King SOLOMON assembled all the people of Israel, and all the elders,
priests and Levites;—and the Levites took up the Ark, and in
grand procession they bore it up to the temple, sacrificing before
it sheep and oxen which could not be told nor numbered for
multitude.   The Levites then delivered it into the hands of the
Priests, who seated it in its place in the Holy of Holies; but the
rest of the multitude did not enter therein, and after that the glory
of the LORD filled the most holy place, none ever entered it but the
High-Priest, and he only once a year, on the great day of expiation.

The Ark was seated on a pedestal prepared for it and placed in
the center of the Holy of Holies.   This pedestal* was a stone rising
there three fingers breadth above the floor, and on either side of it
were the cherubim, fifteen feet high, with their wings expanded so
as to touch the side-walls on each side, and also in the center over
the. Ark.   The Ark was placed with the ends toward the side-
walls, and its side fronting the entrance of the Sanctum Sanctorum,
and the staves being drawn out reached downwards toward the
holy place.†

The Reception and Acknowledgment

WHEN the keystone had been placed in the principal arch, the
temple finished, and the Ark safely seated in the *Sanctum
Sanctorum*, King SOLOMON, having already conferred this honorable
degree upon his most skillful workmen, in further token of his
satisfaction at the successful conclusion of their labors, publicly
received and acknowledged them as Most Excellent Masters, in
the presence and amid the applause of the assembled people.

* Yoma, c. v. § 2.   Dean Prideaux, Con. vol. i. p. 245.   This was not the
Masonic Stone of Foundation, as has been erroneously supposed by some
writers.

† In respect to the Ark there is to be found a wide-spread error.   Most
persons suppose the staves by which the Ark was borne on the shoulders of the
Levites were placed on the sides of the Ark lengthwise; but such was not the
fact.   The staves were fixed across the ends, making the distance between
them three feet and nine inches, instead of two feet and three inches, which
would have been the distance if they had been placed the other way.   See
Prideaux, Con., vol. i. p. 246, for a full confirmation of this fact.

The following Ode is sung:

All hail to the morning, that bids us re - joice;

The tem-ple's com-plet-ed, ex - alt high each voice, The

cap-stone is fin ished, our la - bor is o'er, The

sound of the gav - el shall hail us no more. To the

pow - er Almigh - ty, who ev - er has guid - ed The

tribes of old Is - rael, ex - alt - ing their fame;

To him who hath governed our hearts un - di - vid - ed,

Let's send forth our voi - ces to praise his great name.

Companions, assemble
On this joyful day;
(The occasion is glorious,)
The key-stone to lay;
Fulfill'd is the promise,
By the ANCIENT OF DAYS,
To bring forth the cap-stone
With shouting and praise.

There is no more occasion for level or plumb-line,
 For trowel or gavel, for compass or square;
Our works are completed, the ARK safely seated,
 And we shall be greeted as workmen most rare.

Now those that are worthy,
 Our toils who have shared,
And proved themselves faithful,
 Shall meet their reward.
Their virtue and knowledge,
 Industry and skill,
Have our approbation,
 Have gained our good will.

We accept and receive them, Most Excellent Masters,
 Invested with honors, and power to preside;
Among worthy craftsmen, wherever assembled,
 The knowledge of Masons to spread far and wide.

Almighty Jehovah,
 Descend now and fill
This Lodge with thy glory,
 Our hearts with good-will!
Preside at our meetings,
 Assist us to find
True pleasure in teaching
 Good-will to mankind.

Thy *wisdom* inspired the great institution,
    Thy *strength* shall support it till Nature expire;
And when the creation shall fall into ruin,
    Its *beauty* shall rise through the midst of the fire.

The following passages of Scripture are introduced, accompanied with solemn ceremonies:

The LORD hath said that he would dwell in the thick darkness. But I have built an house of habitation for thee and a place for thy dwelling forever.

And the king turned his face, and blessed the whole congregation of Israel: (and all the congregation of Israel stood:) and he said,

Blessed be the LORD GOD of Israel, who hath with his hands fulfilled that which he spake with his mouth to my father DAVID, saying, Since the day that I brought forth my people out of the land of Egypt, I chose no city among all the tribes of Israel to build an house in, that my name might be there; neither chose I any man to be a ruler over my people Israel; but I have chosen Jerusalem, that my name might be there; and have chosen DAVID to be over my people Israel. Now it was in the heart of DAVID, my father, to build an house for the name of the LORD GOD of

Israel. But the LORD said to DAVID, my father, Forasmuch as it was in thine heart to build an house for my name, thou didst well in that it was in thine heart; notwithstanding, thou shalt not build the house; but thy son, which shall come forth out of thy loins, he shall build the house for my name. The LORD, therefore, hath performed his word that he hath spoken; for I am risen up in the room of DAVID, my father, and am set on the throne of Israel, as the LORD promised, and have built the house for the name of the LORD GOD of Israel; and in it I have put the ark, wherein is the covenant of the LORD, that he made with the children of Israel.

* * * * * *

And he stood before the altar of the LORD, in the presence of all the congregation of Israel, and spread forth his hands; for SOLOMON had made a brazen scaffold of five cubits long, and five cubits broad, and three cubits high, and had set it in the midst of the court; and upon it he stood, and kneeled down upon his knees, before all the congregation of Israel, and spread forth his hands toward heaven, and said,

O LORD GOD of Israel, there is no GOD like thee in the heaven nor in the earth, which keepest covenant, and shewest mercy unto thy servants that walk before thee with all their

hearts; thou which hast kept with thy servant
DAVID, my father, that which thou hast promised
him; and spakest with thy mouth, and has
fulfilled it with thine hand, as it is this day.
Now, therefore, O LORD GOD of Israel, keep
with thy servant DAVID, my father, that which
thou hast promised him, saying, There shall not
fail thee a man in my sight to sit upon the
throne of Israel, yet so that thy children take
heed to their way to walk in my law, as thou
hast walked before me. Now, then, O LORD
GOD of Israel, let thy word be verified, which
thou hast spoken unto thy servant DAVID. But
will GOD in very deed dwell with men on
the earth? Behold, heaven and the heaven of
heavens cannot contain thee: how much less
this house which I have built! Have respect.
therefore, to the prayer of thy servant, and to
his supplication, O LORD my GOD, to hearken
unto the cry and prayer which thy servant
prayeth before thee; that thine eyes may be
open upon this house day and night, upon the
place whereof thou hast said that thou wouldst
put thy name there; to hearken unto the prayer
which thy servant prayeth toward this place.
Hearken, therefore, unto the supplications of

thy servant, and of thy people Israel, which they shall make toward this place; hear thou from thy dwelling-place, even from heaven; and, when thou hearest, forgive.

Now, my GOD, let, I beseech thee, thine eyes be open; and let thine ears be attent unto the prayer that is made in this place. Now, therefore, arise, O LORD GOD, into thy resting-place, thou, and the ark of thy strength: let thy priests, O LORD GOD, be clothed with salvation, and let thy saints rejoice in goodness. O LORD GOD, turn not away the face of thine anointed; remember the mercies of DAVID, thy servant.

*   *   *   *   *   *

When SOLOMON had made an end of praying, the fire came down from heaven, and consumed the burnt-offering and the sacrifices; and the glory of the LORD filled the house. And the priests could not enter into the house of the LORD, because the glory of the LORD had filled the LORD's house. And when all the children of Israel saw how the fire came down, and the glory of the LORD upon the house, they bowed themselves with their faces to the ground upon the pavement, and worshiped, and praised the LORD, saying :

FOR HE IS GOOD; FOR HIS MERCY ENDURETH FOREVER.

*   *   *   *   *   *

THE FIRE FROM HEAVEN

THE fire that consumed the burnt sacrifices of the Jewish nation was first kindled upon the altar "from out from before the LORD,' that is from Heaven, at the time when AARON offered his first sacrifice after his consecration to the High-Priesthood.* From that time this heaven-lighted fire was never suffered to go out, but was kept continually burning on the altar by the direct command of GOD.† When the temple was completed, and the ark seated beneath the wings of the cherubim, the cloud of glory filled the Holy of Holies; and after SOLOMON had finished that fervent and most sublime prayer to JEHOVAH, the sacred fire again came down from Heaven and consumed the offerings of SOLOMON.

This sacred fire was jealously watched by the priests, and kept constantly burning upon the Temple Altar as the first had been on the Altar of the Tabernacle service.‡

* Leviticus, ix. 24.   † Leviticus, vi. 9, 13.

‡ The reference to the Queen of Sheba which has been extensively used in this country within the last thirty or forty years was undoubtedly an innovation of the late Jeremy L. Cross. It is not to be found in any of the earlier rituals, and, indeed, no allusion to it can be found prior to about the year 1817. I have the most indisputable evidence that it was not used in 1795, and for several years later. The visit of the Queen of Sheba to Jerusalem occurred about

In the Lodge this vestal fire is symbolically kept burning on our altar, and in our hearts. "Religion rears the altar and a beam from the throne of GOD wraps it in flame." Hand in hand we gather around that blazing altar and chant the hymn of Masonic charity. We bow in solemn adoration. A scroll of woven light is unfolded by an unseen hand, and on it, written in letters of glowing radiance, we behold the grand aim of our Institution, the end of all its teachings—Glory to GOD, and Love to Man.

———◆———

*   *   *   *   *   *

HISTORICAL SUMMARY

*   *   *   *   *   Alludes to the wonder and admiration expressed by those of our ancient brethren who were permitted to view the interior of that magnificent edifice which King SOLOMON had erected, but more especially to the admiration and astonishment of those who beheld the sublime manifestations of the Supreme Being at the dedication of the temple, when the fire came down from heaven and con-

thirteen years after the consecration of the temple, and, therefore, it is an anachronism to connect that visit with the ceremonies of a degree commemorative of the dedication. Not only so, but it is utterly inconsistent with the whole genius of Masonry to ascribe the origin of any of our mystic rites to one of a Gentile race, and that one too a female. The tradition is, therefore, chronologically incorrect, as applied to the ceremonies of this degree; it is inconsistent with the genius and spirit of the Institution which never goes out into pagan and fetish nations for its rites and ceremonies; it is not to be found in the earlier rituals; and, finally, it is absurdly tame and weak in comparison with those sublime conceptions which are awakened at the allusion to that memorable occasion when, to the astonished gaze of the awe-struck Israelites, the flame descended from the very throne of the Eternal, and consumed the sacrifices. Well might the people evince their admiration and astonishment at such an evidence of Jehovah's presence among them.

sumed the burnt-offering and the sacrifices, and the glory of the LORD filled the LORD's house.

The ceremonies of this degree are intended to represent those of the completion and dedication of King SOLOMON's Temple. You have now arrived at a period of Masonry when the labor is over. The key-stone has been placed in the principal arch, the temple finished, and the ark, which has been so long without a resting-place, has been at length safely seated.

We have imitated our ancient brethren in assembling on that occasion, repairing to the place designated, and participating in those solemn ceremonies. We have imitated them in gathering around the altar, engaging in prayer, and have witnessed a representation of the fire coming down from heaven, consuming the burnt-offering and the sacrifices. We have also imitated their astonishment on beholding it, by falling down upon the ground and exclaiming: "He is good; for his mercy endureth forever!"

A perusal of the books of Chronicles and Kings will give you a minute description of the temple and * * * * * * * * *

You will there find that the foundations of

the temple were laid by King SOLOMON in the year of the world 2992, and the building was finished in the year 3000.

About seven years and six months were consumed in its erection.

It was dedicated in the year 3001, with the most imposing and solemn ceremonies, to the worship of Jehovah, who condescended to make it the place for the special manifestation of his glory. The ceremonies lasted fourteen days. Seven days of this festival were devoted to the dedication exclusively, and seven to the Feast of the Tabernacle.

This structure, for magnificence, beauty, and expense, exceeded any building that was ever erected. It was built of large stones of white marble, curiously hewn, and so artfully joined together that they appeared like one entire stone. Its roof was of olive wood, covered with gold; and when the sun shone thereon, the reflection from it was of such refulgent splendor, that it dazzled the eyes of all who beheld it. Its various courts and other apartments were capable of holding three hundred thousand persons It was adorned with 1,453 columns, of the finest Parian marble, twisted, sculptured, and voluted; and 2,906 pilasters, decorated with magnificent capitals. The oracle and sanctuary were lined with massive gold, adorned with embellishments in sculpture, and set with numerous, gorgeous, and dazzling decorations of diamonds and all kinds of precious stones. In the emphatic language of JOSEPHUS, " the temple shone and dazzled the eyes of such as entered it by the splendor of the gold that was on every side of them."

The multitude on beholding it were struck with bewildering amazement, and raised their hands in admiration and astonishment at its wondrous magnificence, as well as to protect their eyes from the effect of its exceeding brilliancy.

Nothing ever equaled the splendor of its consecration. Israel sent forth her thousands, and the assembled people beheld, in solemn adoration, the vast sacrifice of SOLOMON accepted. The flame descended upon the altar and consumed the offering; the shadow and glory of the Eternal proclaimed his presence between the cherubim, and the voice of his thunders told to the faithful of the Craft that the perfectness of their labor was approved.

* * * * Bright was the hour
When Israel's princes, in their pride and power,
Knelt in the temple's court; the living flame
The accepted sacrifice to all proclaim.
Brightly the splendor of the Godhead shone,
In awful glory, from his living throne;
Then bowed was every brow—no human sight
Could brave the splendor of that flood of light
That vailed his presence and his awful form—
Whose path the whirlwind is—whose breath the storm.

Our mystic temple is now completed and dedicated. You have wrought more than seven years with zeal and fidelity, and have been received and acknowledged as a Most Excellent Master. You are now invested with power to travel into foreign countries, work and receive Master's wages, and dispense Masonic light and knowledge to all uninformed brethren.

The temple which we have just completed represents the temple of the present life. The foreign country into which, after its completion, a Mason is expected to travel, is that "undiscovered country from whose bourne no traveler returns." The wages which he is to receive are the rewards of a well-spent life and the knowledge of divine truth, which the Grand Master of the Universe will bestow upon all who have faithfully performed their task.

You have seen the foundations of the temple laid deep and strong. You have, as an Entered Apprentice, served your Master with freedom, fervency, and zeal; and, as a bearer of burdens, have brought up from the quarries of Zarthan many a rough ashlar for the building. You have wrought your full time as a Fellow-Craft, and, under the skillful touch of your working tools, these rough ashlars have become perfect ashlars—stones, we doubt not, fitted to adorn and beautify our temple. As a Master-workman, you have watched with unceasing care the wondrous beauties of the temple increase under the skillful hands of the Widow's Son; and now you have at length seen the object of our hopes completed, and the last arch bound together by the rejected though priceless key-stone.

We have now dedicated the temple to the service of the Supreme Being; and by this we are reminded that we should also dedicate our spiritual building—that temple which we have been erecting within ourselves—to the service of the same Supreme Being. And although we know of a certainty that all earthly things are transient, and that in process of time, even at the best, the decay of ages will crumble our magnificent temple into dust, yet we are persuaded, that, if we have erected the temple of our inner life by Square, Plumb-Line, and Rule, its foundations shall never fail, and its fabric shall never crumble nor decay. Then let us, my brother, take care that we so labor in the erection of our temple here, that when we leave this, for that far-distant country from whence we shall never return, we may there receive the wages of faithful craftsmen.

CHARGE TO THE CANDIDATE

BROTHER: Your admission to this degree of Masonry is a proof of the good opinion the brethren of this Lodge entertain of your Masonic abilities. Let this consideration induce you to be careful of forfeiting, by misconduct and inattention to our rules, that esteem which has raised you to the rank which you now possess.

It is one of your great duties, as a Most Excellent Master, to dispense light and truth to the uninformed Mason; and I need not remind you of the impossibility of complying with this obligation without possessing an accurate acquaintance with the lectures of each degree.

If you are not already completely conversant in all the degrees heretofore conferred on you, remember that an indulgence, prompted by a belief that you will apply yourself with double diligence to make yourself so, has induced the brethren to accept you. Let it, therefore, be your unremitting study to acquire such a degree of knowledge and information, as shall enable you to discharge with propriety the various duties incumbent on you, and to preserve, unsullied, the title now conferred upon you of a Most Excellent Master.

———•———

CLOSING

*   *   *   *   *   *

THE following Psalm is read at CLOSING:

The LORD is my shepherd; I shall not want. He maketh me to lie down in green pastures; he leadeth me beside the still waters. He restoreth my soul; he leadeth me in the paths of righteousness for his name's sake. Yea. though I walk through the valley of the shadow of death, I will fear no evil; for thou art with me; thy rod and thy staff, they comfort me. Thou preparest a table before me, in the presence of mine enemies; thou anointest my head with oil; my cup runneth over. Surely goodness and mercy shall follow me all the days of my life; and I will dwell in the house of the LORD forever.

Or the following may be used:

PRAYER

O GOD, our Creator, Preserver, and Benefactor, unto whom all hearts are open, and all desires known, and from whom no secrets are hid; we heartily thank thee for the fraternal communion we have now been permitted to enjoy. Watch over our Institution and make it an instrument of great good in the world. Go with us, we beseech thee as we separate. Guide us evermore by thy good Providence; and finally reunite us all, in the glorious temple above, to praise thee forever.

Response. So mote it be.—AMEN.

KING SOLOMON'S TEMPLE

THIS famous fabric was situated on Mount Moriah, a lofty hill almost in the north-east corner of Jerusalem. At a little distance to the south-west was Mount Zion with the city of David and the king's palace on its summit. The top of Moriah was almost a square, occupying about five hundred cubits on each side, and was enclosed by a wall twelve and a half yards high. This was the place, it is said, where ABRA- HAM was about to offer up his son ISAAC, and also where DAVID met and appeased the destroying angel who was visible over the threshing floor of ORNAN the Jebusite. To prepare the place for the foundations of the building, it was first surrounded with an immense wall, and the space between the wall and the summit was filled in and made solid with large stones of almost incredible size. On this foundation were laid other stones firmly morticed into the rock, so as to furnish a secure basis for the building proper.

King SOLOMON commenced the erection of the temple on the second day of the month Zif, in the year of the world 2992. It was the fourth year of his reign, being four hundred and eighty years after the passage of the Red Sea, and the work was carried on with such prodigious speed that it was finished in all its parts in little more than seven years.

The building does not appear to have been remarkable for its size, as many temples in Egypt and other heathen countries then existing, exceeded it in magnitude. Its surpassing ex- cellence over all other structures consisted in its cost and the magnificence of its decorations. Built of enormous blocks of white marble, put together with all the architectural symmetry and harmony which the most ingenious workmen could devise, it was a monument of skill and mechanical ability. The roof, beams, doors, posts, and gates were overlaid with the gold of Ophir, and so, its effulgence dazzled all who beheld it.

The temple was situated due East and West, the Holy of Holies being in the West end, and the porch or entrance toward the East. The length was 70 cubits, or about 105 feet; the width was 20 cubits, or about 30 feet. But this does not include the chambers and courts around the temple proper, for these, it must be remembered, were capable of holding 300,000 persons. The temple proper was divided into three separate or distinct apartments: the porch, the holy place or sanctuary, and the Holy of Holies or *Sanctum Sanctorum*. The porch was 10 cubits long, from East to West, and 120 cubits* high. The sanctuary was 40 cubits long, and the *Sanctum Sanctorum* 20 cubits. In the latter apartment or portion of the building was placed the Ark of the Covenant containing the tables of stone, AARON's rod, and the pot of manna. In the sanctuary were placed the golden candlestick, the table of shew bread, and the altar of incense. The entrance from the porch into the sanctuary was through a wide door of olive posts and leaves of fir; but the door between the sanctuary and the Holy of Holies was composed entirely of olive wood. These doors were always open, and the aperture closed by a suspended curtain. The partition between the sanctuary and the Holy of Holies was partly composed of an open net-work, so that the incense daily offered in the former place might be diffused through this net-work into the latter.

As before remarked, the temple proper was surrounded by various courts and high walls, which occupied together the entire summit of Mount Moriah. The first or outer court was the Court of the Gentiles, beyond which no Gentile was allowed to pass. Within this, and separated from it by a low wall, was the Court of the Children of Israel, and within that, and separated from it by another wall, was the Court of the Priests, in which was placed the altar of burnt offerings. From this court there was an ascent of twelve steps to the porch of the temple proper, before which stood the two brazen pillars Jachin and Boaz.

The vessels consecrated to the perpetual use of the temple, were suited to the magnificence of the edifice in which they were deposited and used. JOSEPHUS states that there were one hundred and forty thousand of those vessels which were

---

* The *Ammah* or cubit was derived from the distance from the elbow to the extremity of the middle finger. Little information is furnished by the Bible itself as to the absolute length of the cubit, although it is frequently mentioned. Scholars have never yet settled the question whether there were two or three different measures represented by the term, but it is generally agreed that there were at least two. The length of the common cubit is generally conceded to have been about eighteen inches.

made of gold; and one million three hundred and forty thousand of silver; ten thousand vestments for the priests, made of silk, with purple girdles; and two millions of purple vestments for the singers. There were also two hundred thousand trumpets, and forty thousand musical instruments, made use of in the temple, and in worshiping GOD.

The dedication ceremonies were indescribably grand and imposing. "Magnificent must have been the sight, to see the young king, clothed in royalty, officiating as priest before the immense altar, while the thousands of Levites and priests on the east side, habited in surplices, with harps, cymbals, and trumpets in their hands, led the eye to the beautiful pillars flanking the doors of the temple now thrown open and displaying the interior brilliantly lighted up; while the burnished gold of the floor, the ceiling, and the walls, with the precious gems with which they were enriched, reflecting the light on all sides, would completely overwhelm the imagination, were it not excited by the view of the embroidered vail, to consider the yet more awful glories of the Most Holy Place. And astounding must have been the din of the instruments of the four thousand Levites, led on by the priests with one hundred and twenty trumpets, directing the chorusses of the immense congregation, as they chanted the sublime compositions of the royal psalmist, in the grand intonations of the Hebrew language, like the roaring of many waters."*

The Temple of SOLOMON has been symbolized in many different ways, and a Mason who has studied the sublime lessons inculcated in the several degrees until he has reached the distinguished rank of a Most Excellent Master, cannot fail to discover much valuable truth in the history of the temple. In the superb glory of the building, and the gorgeous ceremonies of its dedication, the true craftsman sees the symbols of the spiritual temple with its golden streets. Around and about him are the signs of decay, and death, which cling with awful tenacity to his degenerate nature. But these are Masonic shadows of supernal gladness; and the eye of faith looks through them to that light which "shineth more and more unto the perfect day."

* Bardwell's Temples, p. 87.

ROYAL ARCH

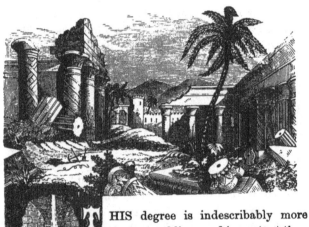

THIS degree is indescribably more august, sublime, and important than all which precede it; and is the summit and perfection of ancient Masonry. It impresses on our minds a belief of the being and existence of a Supreme Deity, without beginning of days or end of years, and reminds us of the reverence due to his holy name. It also brings to light many essentials of the Craft, which were, for the space of four hundred and seventy years, buried in darkness, and without a knowledge of which the Masonic character cannot be complete.

OFFICERS

A CHAPTER of Royal Arch Masons consists of any convenient number of members, and the following officers, viz:

1. The HIGH-PRIEST, whose title is "Most Excellent," represents JOSHUA, the first High-Priest of the Jews, after their return from the Babylonish captivity. He is seated in the East, and is dressed in a robe of blue, purple. scarlet, and white, and is decorated with the ephod, breast-plate and miter—the garments and decorations of the ancient High-Priest of the Jews. On the front of the miter, upon a golden plate, is inscribed, in Hebrew characters, *Holiness to the Lord.* His jewel is a miter. The use of a Pontifical or Roman Catholic miter, instead of the miter of the Jewish High-Priest, is entirely incorrect.

2. The KING, whose title is "Excellent," represents ZERUBBABEL, a Prince of Judah, who was the leader of the first colony of Jews that returned from the Babylonish captivity to rebuild the temple. His station is in the East, on the right of the High-Priest, clothed in a scarlet robe, with a crown on his head and a scepter in his hand. His jewel is a level, surmounted by a crown.

3. The SCRIBE, whose title is "Excellent," represents Haggai the prophet. His station is in the East, on the left of the High-Priest, clothed in a purple robe, and wearing a turban of the same color. His jewel is a plumb, surmounted by a turban. These three officers constitute the Grand Council.

4. The CAPTAIN OF THE HOST represents the General of the troops who returned from Babylon. His station is in front, on the right of the Council. He wears a white robe and helmet; and is armed with a sword. His jewel is a triangular plate, on which an armed soldier is engraved.

5. The PRINCIPAL SOJOURNER represents the leader of a party of Jews, who sojourned in Babylon for a time after the departure of ZERUBBABEL with the main body, and who subsequently came up to Jerusalem to assist in rebuilding the temple. He wears a black robe, with a rose-colored border, and a slouched hat and pilgrim's staff. His station is on the left, in front of the Council. His jewel is a triangular plate, on which a pilgrim is engraved.

6. The ROYAL ARCH CAPTAIN represents the Captain of the King's guards. He wears a white robe, and cap or helmet, and is armed with a sword. His station is in front of the Council, and at the entrance of the fourth vail. His jewel is a sword.

7. The GRAND MASTER OF THE THIRD VAIL sits at the entrance of the third vail, the color of which is scarlet. He wears a scarlet robe and turban. His jewel is a sword.

8. The GRAND MASTER OF THE SECOND VAIL sits at the entrance of the second vail, the color of which is purple. He wears a purple robe and turban. His jewel is a sword.

9. The GRAND MASTER OF THE FIRST VAIL sits at the entrance of the first vail, the color of which is blue. He wears a blue robe and turban. His jewel is a sword.

These three officers represent the guards of the Tabernacle, and especially those who were exalted to that rank to guard a valuable treasure, a duty for which their industry, zeal, and fidelity had qualified them.

The TREASURER, SECRETARY and TILER occupy their respective positions as in previous degrees, and wear their appropriate jewels.

According to the English ritual, the first officer represents ZERUBBABEL, the second HAGGAI, and the third JOSHUA, an arrangement which Dr. OLIVER admits is incorrect; but he suggests a change open to equally strong objections as exist against their present system. He and other English writers prefer that the order should be ZERUBBABEL, JOSHUA, HAGGAI, because they say that the Messiah entered first upon the prophetical office; then on the sacerdotal at Golgotha; and, lastly, on the regal at Olivet. But this argument proves too much, if anything; for, according to that, our English companions should place HAGGAI first and ZERUBBABEL last.

It has been said that the Americans made an innovation at this point, during the latter part of the last century, on account of their hatred of the kingly office, an imputation which is wholly undeserved by the fathers of Masonry in the United States. A careful consideration of the Jewish polity, and the evidently typical design of the threefold offices in the Grand Council of the Chapter, will convince any candid inquirer after truth that the American or WEBB Ritual can be sustained on the plainest grounds of common sense, historical correctness, and sound symbolism, while the English can be defended on neither. It is well known to every reader that under the patriarchal form of government by which the Hebrews were ruled, until after the exodus from Egypt, the Patriarch united in himself the threefold office of Priest, King, and Prophet, and in that respect was a type of the Messiah. When GOD, in his wisdom, determined to bring his people out from the "house of bondage," and destined them to become a great and powerful nation, he then gave them a code of laws and set over them a gorgeous hierarchy, endowed with special privileges and invested with a pomp and splendor befitting their high calling as Priests of the Most High GOD.

To this Priesthood was annexed not only the prophetical office, but also the regal, inasmuch as the High-Priest, until the election of SAUL as King of Israel, was also the judge of the nation. And even after the Almighty had, in compliance with their importunities, consented to give his people a king, still the High-Priest continued to be in fact the head and front of the nation, an officer of far greater influence and power than the king. The High-Priest still remained the prime minister under GOD for their government, who, in all matters of moment, consulted GOD what was to be done, and so ruled the nation.[*]

It is universally conceded by all intelligent Jews that in the temple, and all its concerns, the High-Priest was superior to the king. "A fact," says a Jewish Mason, "which proves that the companions in the United States had a more correct knowledge of the Israelitish Institutions than Dr. OLIVER."[†]

Again the first three Officers of a Chapter are universally considered, as well by Jew as Christian Masons, to be symbolical of the threefold offices of the Messiah. The Jew applies them, it is true, to a Messiah yet to come, but this does not militate against the symbolism.

Although the Messiah unites the three offices of Priest, King, and Prophet, yet for the great purpose of man's redemption we look mainly to his sacerdotal office. That is the prominent central feature of his life, the great end of his death. Our love for the Messiah clusters around that great sacrifice; and the idea suggested to our minds by the mention of his name is the offering made by him in the character of the Great High-Priest of our salvation.

To set up in our Chapters the kingly office, the symbol of earthly rulership, above the sanctity of the High-Priesthood, is to innovate on the plainest facts in the Jewish polity, destroy the finest symbolism to be found in the threefold offices of the Chapter, and do violence to our ideas of natural propriety.

It has also been urged that the use of the word Scribe, as applied to HAGGAI, is incorrect. The word is of frequent use in the Scriptures, and is applied by Hebrew writers to the minor prophets. In this sense it is used in connection with HAGGAI.

[*] Patrick. Com., vol. i., p. 266.

[†] L. Hynemann. Mirror and Keystone, vol. iv., p. 103.

JEWELS AND CLOTHING

THE jewels of a Chapter are of gold or yellow metal, suspended within a triangle.

The symbolic color of this degree is scarlet.

The collar and sash of a Royal Arch Mason are scarlet, edged with gold.

The apron is of white lambskin, lined and bound with scarlet; on the flap of which should be placed a triple tau within a triangle, and all within a circle.

Chapters of Royal Arch Masons are "dedicated to ZERUBBABEL."

Candidates receiving this degree are said to be "exalted to the most sublime degree of the Royal Arch."

A Royal Arch Chapter represents the Tabernacle erected by our ancient brethren near the ruins of King SOLOMON'S Temple.

The Triple Tau

Is formed by the junction of three tau crosses, T, so called from their resemblance to the letter tau of the Greeks.

This emblem was early appropriated to the Royal Arch, but its origin and meaning has never been satisfactorily explained. In England it is called the "grand emblem of Royal Arch Masonry," and the English lectures thus explain it: "The triple tau forms two right angles on each side of the exterior lines, and another at the center, by their union; for the three angles of each triangle are equal to two right angles. This being triplified illustrates the jewel worn by the Companions of the Royal Arch ; which, by its intersection, forms a given number of angles, that may be taken in five several combinations; and reduced, their amount in right angles will be found equal to the five Platonic bodies which represent the four elements and the sphere of the universe." Some have supposed this emblem to be an allusion to the three Great Lights of Masonry; others interpret it to be the letters H. T., the initials of Hiram of Tyre, or those of *Templum Hierosolymae*, the Temple of Jerusalem; while others assert that it is only a modification of the Hebrew letter *Schin*, ש. Perhaps its true signification may be the following: The device on the banner of the tribe of LEVI is supposed to have been a dagger. The triple tau, or three daggers, may be emblematic of the three offices into which the children of LEVI were installed, and to which they were set apart by the command of GOD, viz., High-Priest, Priests and Levites.

However this may be, the true symbolism of the triple tau undoubtedly is to represent the sacred name of the *Great I Am*, and as such was appropriately adopted by Royal Arch Masons as an emblem to designate those who have been taught the sublime secrets of that august degree.

THE LECTURE

OF this degree is divided into two sections, and should be well understood by every Royal Arch Mason; upon an accurate acquaintance with it will depend his usefulness at our assemblies; and without it he will be unqualified to perform the duties of the various stations in which his services may be required by the Chapter.

SECTION FIRST

This section explains the mode of government and organization of a Chapter; it designates the appellation, number and situation of the several officers, and points out the purposes and duties of their respective stations.

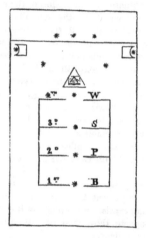

OPENING

* * * * * *

DEVOTIONS

OUR FATHER, who art in heaven, hallowed be thy name. Thy kingdom come. Thy will be done on earth as it is in heaven. Give us this day our daily bread. And forgive us our trespasses, as we forgive those who trespass against us. And lead us not into temptation; but deliver us from evil: For thine is the kingdom, and the power, and the glory, forever and ever. AMEN.

*   *   *   *   *   *

CHARGE AT OPENING

Now we command you, Brethren, that ye withdraw yourselves from every brother that walketh disorderly, and not after the tradition which ye received of us. For yourselves know how ye ought to follow us ; for we behaved not ourselves disorderly among you. Neither did we eat any man's bread for nought; but wrought with labor and travail night and day, that we might not be chargeable to any of you; not because we have not power, but to make ourselves an ensample unto you to follow us. For even when we were with you, this we commanded you, that if any would not work, neither should he eat. For we hear that there are some which walk among you disorderly, working not at all, but are busy-bodies. Now them that are such, we command and exhort, that with quietness they work, and eat their own bread. But ye, Brethren, be not weary in well-doing. And if any man obey not our word by this epistle, note that man, and have no company with him, that he may be ashamed. Yet count him not as an enemy, but admonish him as a brother. Now the LORD of peace himself give you peace always by all means. The LORD be with you all.—II. THESS., iii., 6-16.

* * * * * *

* * * * *

SECTION SECOND

This section is fully supplied with illustrations of historical truth. It amplifies, in beautiful and striking colors, that prosperity and happiness are the sure attendants of perseverance and justice; while dishonor and ruin invariably follow the practice of vice and immorality. It contains much that is beautifully illustrative of the preceding degrees; a perfect knowledge of which is essential to the accomplished and well-informed Mason.

THE FIRST CLAUSE furnishes us with many interesting particulars relative to the state of the Fraternity during and since the reign of King SOLOMON ; and illustrates the causes and consequences of some very important events which occurred during his reign.

RECEPTION

* * * * * *

* * * * * *

THE following passages of Scripture, with Prayer, are introduced during the ceremony of exaltation:

I will bring the blind by a way that they knew not; I will lead them in paths that they have not known; I will make darkness light before them, and crooked things straight. These things will I do unto them, and not forsake them.

* * * * * *

At every stage in Masonry great moral truths are presented to the neophyte and enforced by impressive lessons. So here, at the very threshold of this most sublime degree, we are taught to put our trust in the Name of the LORD, and are assured that whatever may befall us, the Lion of the tribe of Judah will not forsake us. By his power, when all human efforts failed, we were raised; and now, in our search for further light, we are taught that if we put our whole trust in him, we shall not be cast down; for, although we may be led through the valley of the shadow of death, yet we shall not perish.

*　　　*　　　*　　　*　　　*　　　*

He that humbleth himself shall be exalted

*　　　*　　　*　　　*　　　*　　　*

Humility is a virtue absolutely essential to an earnest seeker after truth. The Mason who would successfully prosecute his inquiries into the mysterious ways of nature, or make any progress toward the sublime truths which underlie the great fabric of Freemasonry, must, at the very outset of his investigations, lay aside all pride of learning, and all worldly arrogance, and, clad in the sable garb of humility, seek for the brightest manifestations of truth deep down among the lowly. The candidate, having been already taught to put his trust in GOD, is, therefore, reminded that a knowledge of truth is only attained after humble and patient search, and he is commanded to stoop low; for "he that humbleth himself shall be exalted."

The *Catenarian Arch* made use of in this degree by some writers is evidently an innovation. A due consideration of the lecture will enable us to avoid this modern error. There can be but one form to the Royal Arch, and a due attention to this subject will insure not only strict propriety and solemnity in the ceremonies, but also a correct knowledge of the beautiful symbolism intended to be taught.

We are consequently instructed to make a proper use of our sublime secrets, and to communicate them only in the ancient mode; and more, we learn to begin every important undertaking by looking to the Deity for aid and support.

*　　　*　　　*　　　*　　　*　　　*

PRAYER

O THOU eternal and omnipotent Jehovah, the glorious and everlasting I AM, permit us, thy frail, dependent, and needy creatures, in the name of our *Most Excellent and Supreme High-Priest*, to approach thy divine Majesty. And do thou, who sittest *between the Cherubim*, incline thine ear to the voice of our praises and of our supplication: and vouchsafe to commune with us from off the *mercy seat*. We humbly adore and worship thy unspeakable perfections, and thy unbounded goodness and benevolence. We bless thee, that when man had sinned, and fallen from his innocence and happiness, thou didst still leave unto him the powers of reasoning and the capacity of improvement and of pleasure. We adore thee, that amidst the pains and calamities of our present state, so many means of refreshment and satisfaction are afforded us, while traveling the *rugged path of life*. And O thou who didst aforetime appear unto thy servant MOSES, *in a flame of fire, out of the midst of a bush*, enkindle, we beseech thee, in each of our hearts, a flame of devotion to thee, of love to each other, and of benevolence and charity to all mankind. May the *vails* of ignorance and blindness be removed from the eyes of our understandings, that we may behold and adore thy mighty and wondrous works. May the *rod* and staff of thy grace and power continually support us and defend us from the rage of all our enemies, and especially from the subtility and malice of that old *serpent*, who, with cruel vigilance, seeketh our ruin. May the *leprosy* of sin be eradicated from our *bosoms*, and may *Holiness to the Lord* be engraven upon all our thoughts, words, and actions. May the *incense* of piety ascend continually unto thee, from off the *altar* of our hearts, and *burn day and night*, as a sweet-smelling savor unto thee. May we daily *search* the records of *truth*, that we may be more and more instructed in our duty; and may we share the blessedness of those who hear the *sacred word and keep it.* And, finally, O merciful Father, when we shall have passed through the outward *vails* of these earthly *courts*, when the earthly house of this *Taber-nacle* shall be dissolved, may we be admitted into the *Holy of Holies* above, into the presence of the *Grand Council* of Heaven, where the Supreme *High-Priest* forever presides—forever reigns.·

AMEN.—So mote it be.

The posture of prayer among the Jews was mostly standing, but when the occasion was one of especial solemnity or humiliation, it was naturally expressed by kneeling. In the latter posture alone, the foregoing sublime prayer should always be reverently offered.

*   *   *   *   *   *

*   *   *   *   *   *

SILENCE AND SECRECY

MYSTERY has charms as well as power. "The entire fabric of the universe is founded on secrecy; and the great Life-force which vivifies, moves, and beautifies the whole, is the profoundest of all mysteries. We cannot, indeed, fix our eyes on a single point in creation which does not shade off into mystery and touch the realms of Eternal Silence."

The first obligation of a Mason—his supreme duty—his chief virtue—is that of silence and secrecy. This primary duty is particularly enforced in this degree; and along with it are likewise inculcated, in the most solemn manner, the three-fold duties which Royal Arch Masons owe to GOD, to their fellow beings, and to themselves. No one that deserves the name can ever forget the ties of a Royal Arch Mason. And if the lesson is heeded the initiate must become a true friend, a pure patriot, and a better man.

*   *   *   *   *   *

Now Moses kept the flock of JETHRO, his father-in-law, the priest of Midian; and he led the flock to the back side of the desert, and came to the mountain of GOD. even to Horeb. And the Angel of the LORD appeared unto him in a flame of fire, out of the midst of a bush; and he looked, and behold the bush burned

with fire, and the bush was not consumed. And MOSES said, I will now turn aside and see this great sight, why the bush is not burnt. And when the LORD saw that he turned aside to see, GOD called unto him out of the midst of the bush, and said, MOSES! MOSES! And he said, Here am I. And he said Draw not nigh hither: put off thy shoes from off thy feet, for the place whereon thou standest is holy ground. Moreover, he said, I am the GOD of thy father, the GOD of ABRAHAM, the GOD of ISAAC, and the GOD of JACOB. And MOSES hid his face, for he was afraid to look upon GOD.—EXOD. iii., 1-6.

* * * * * *

As the Royal Arch Mason must make himself thoroughly acquainted with the leading events in the exodus of the children of Israel, if he would understand those instructions which distinguish him from the rest of the Fraternity, it is peculiarly appropriate that his attention should be drawn to that passage of Scripture which relates the circumstances under which the Jewish law-giver was commissioned by the Almighty to conduct the children of Israel out from the land of Egypt.

It was in the seclusion and simplicity of his shepherd life that MOSES received his call as a prophet. The traditional scene of this great event is in the valley of Shoayb, on the north side of Jebel Mûsa, or Mount Horeb. Upon the mountain was the well-known acacia or shittim tree, the thorn tree of the desert, spreading out its tangled branches, thick set with white thorns, over the rocky ground. It was this tree which became the symbol of Divine Presence; a flame of fire in the midst of it, in which the dry branches would have naturally crackled and burnt in a moment, but which played around it without consuming it. The rocky ground at once became holy, and that it might not be polluted, MOSES was commanded to put off his shepherd's sandals. Removing the shoes was an ancient custom of general practice in performing religious rites. The Jewish priesthood sacrificed with bare feet. The Cretans made it penal for any person to enter the Temple of Diana with covered feet; and even the Roman ladies of the highest rank were not excused from this requirement when they entered the Temple of Vesta. This custom is still preserved among the nations of the East. A learned writer thus symbolizes the lesson of the Burning Bush: "As MOSES was commanded to pull his shoes from off his feet, on Mount Horeb, because the ground whereon he trod was sanctified by the presence of the Divinity; so the Mason who would prepare himself for this august stage of Masonry should advance in the path of truth, be divested of every degree of arrogance, and come as a true Acacian, or blameless worshiper, with innocence, humility, and virtue, to challenge the ensigns of an Order, whose institutions are founded on the most sacred principles of religion."

    *   *   *   *   *   *

ZEDEKIAH was one-and-twenty years old when he began to reign, and reigned eleven years in Jerusalem. And he did that which was evil in the sight of the LORD his GOD, and humbled not himself before JEREMIAH the prophet speaking from the mouth of the LORD.

And he also rebelled against King NEBUCHAD-NEZZAR, and stiffened his neck, and hardened his heart, from turning unto the LORD GOD of Israel. Moreover, all the chief of the priests, and the people, transgressed very much after all the abominations of the heathen, and polluted the house of the LORD, which he had hallowed in Jerusalem. And the LORD GOD of their fathers sent to them by his messengers, because he had compassion on his people and on his dwelling-place. But they mocked the messengers of God, and despised his words and misused his prophets, until the wrath of the Lord arose against his people, till there was no remedy.

Therefore he brought upon them the King of the Chaldees, who slew their young men with the sword in the house of their sanctuary, and had no compassion upon young man or maiden, old men, or him that stooped for age; he gave them all into his hand. And all the vessels of the house of God, great and small, and the treasures of the house of the Lord, and the treasures of the king, and of his princes; all these he brought to Babylon. And they burnt the house of God, and brake down the wall of Jerusalem, and burnt all the palaces thereof with fire, and destroyed all the goodly vessels thereof. And them that had escaped from the sword carried he away to Babylon; where they were servants to him and his sons, until the reign of the kingdom of Persia.

How solemn and mournful in its sublimity is this description! We have followed the history of God's people step by step, commencing with their exodus from Egypt. We have seen the miraculous interposition of the Almighty in their behalf, on the banks of the Red Sea, in the wilderness, and on many a battle-field. We have seen the Jewish people increase in power, riches, and glory, until the splendor of their chief city and capital rivaled, if it did not surpass, all the world in its magnificence. We have

seen the foundations of the temple laid by the wisest king that ever wore a crown, and have watched its rapid progress toward completion, dazzled and amazed at its exuberant beauty and costliness. We have seen the temple completed, the pride and glory of the Hebrew nation, the wonder of the past, the earthly symbol of the heavenly temple of the new Jerusalem. As we turn back to the days of SOLOMON, and see the unexampled prosperity of the nation, the wisdom by which he was inspired, and remember the wondrous protection vouchsafed to his chosen people by GOD, we forget, for the moment, how desperately wicked that people became, how grievously they sinned, and dream that such a people must be happy. But, alas! how vain our fancy! How terrible was their punishment! What a crowd of sad emotions rush through our minds as we are recalled to our senses and behold the utter desolation of Jerusalem, and the sack and destruction of the house of the LORD. The miseries of the siege, the rivers of blood poured out in vain to defend the city, the final assault with its awful carnage, the butchery of the old and feeble, the unbridled license and lust of the Chaldean soldiery, the long and dreary march of the captive Hebrews in the triumphal train of NEBUCHAD-NEZZAR, the hardships and terrible trials of the captivity; these, and much more, pass in review before our mental vision, and, like the sons of Israel in a strange land, we weep when we remember Zion.

THE SECOND CLAUSE

Introduces a new era, and is replete with the most valuable information. It inculcates the great virtues of faith and perseverance, and demonstrates that virtue will sooner or later receive its reward. The ceremonies and lessons made use of are inexpressibly grand and imposing, and are well calculated to lead the mind to the praise and adoration of the GREAT I AM.

In the first year of CYRUS, King of Persia, the LORD stirred up the spirit of CYRUS, King of Persia, that he made a proclamation throughout all his kingdom, and put it also in writing.

PROCLAMATION

THUS saith CYRUS, King of Persia, the LORD
GOD of heaven hath given me all the kingdoms
of the earth, and he hath charged me to build
him an house at Jerusalem, which is in Judah.
Who is there among you of all his people? his
GOD be with him, and let him go up to Jerusalem, which is in Judah, and build the house of
the LORD GOD of Israel, (he is the GOD) which
is in Jerusalem.—EZRA i., 2, 3.

The seventy years, which the prophet Jeremiah had foretold
should be the duration of Judah's captivity, were now just expired.
King CYRUS, inspired by GOD, and prompted by the counsels of
DANIEL and the prophecies of ISAIAH, issued his royal decree for
the liberation of the Hebrew captives, in the first year of his reign,
B. C. 536.

With what joy must this proclamation have been heard by the
sons and daughters of Israel, whose harps, hanging on the willows,
had been for seventy years untuned to the songs of Zion! With
what alacrity the children of the captivity, under the lead of the
chief of the fathers, must have girded themselves for their
departure, to rebuild their city and temple!

The principal people of the tribes of Judah and Benjamin, with
the Priests and Levites, to the number of 42,360, having been
supplied by those who remained behind, with many valuable
treasures, and having in charge five thousand and four hundred
holy vessels of gold and silver belonging to the temple, which had
been carried away into Babylon, immediately departed for
Jerusalem.

Among their leaders there are three that deserve especial
mention.

JOSHUA, who was the High-Priest by lineal descent from the
Pontifical family, succeeded to that office on the death of his
father, JOZADAK, who died in Babylon during the captivity. The

latter became High-Priest at the death of SERAIAH, who held that office at the time of the destruction of the temple, and was slain by NEBUCHADNEZZAR at Riblah.

ZERUBBABEL, or SHESHBAZZAR, as he was called in Babylon, was the son of SELATHIEL, the son of Jehoiachin, and the direct lineal successor to the regal office of Judah. He was the acknowledged "Prince of Judah, or Prince of the Captivity." He was also appointed by CYRUS the governor of Judea, and in both of these capacities was the recognized civil leader of the returning captives, as JOSHUA was the ecclesiastical.

HAGGAI, the Scribe, or Prophet, who was associated with the two just mentioned, was, according to tradition, born in Babylon, and was but a young man when he went up to Jerusalem. With regard to his tribe and parentage, both history and tradition are alike silent. He was the first of those who prophesied after the captivity, and on the accession of DARIUS to the throne, by the direction of GOD, incited the people to renew and complete the work on the temple, which had been suspended.

The journey from Babylon to Judea occupied about four months. The Jews left Babylon about the middle of the month Chisleu, and arrived at Jerusalem in the month Nisan.* As soon as they came thither, they dispersed themselves according to their tribes and the families of their fathers, into their several cities, and betook themselves to rebuilding their houses and preparing the land for raising the necessary sustenance.

On the first day of the month Tisri, the people assembled at Jerusalem and celebrated the Feast of Trumpets. Having previously erected a tabernacle and set up the altar, on the tenth of the same month, they kept, with all the ancient solemnities, the great day of Expiation, followed on the fifteenth and succeeding days by the Feast of Tabernacles. The feasts and sacrifices of the Jewish religion having been thus restored, the people at once began to collect the offerings for the rebuilding of the temple.

The foundations of the new edifice were not laid, however, until the month Zif of the following year, the first year being consumed in necessary preparations. During this period the number of the people at Jerusalem was occasionally augmented by the arrival of small parties of those who were left behind in Babylon by the main body under ZERUBBABEL, and who afterward came up to assist their brethren in rebuilding the house of the LORD.

* Dr. Prideaux, Con., vol. i. p. 232.

These small parties were composed mostly of those who were settled in the more remote provinces of the empire, and on that account did not hear the good news contained in the proclamation of CYRUS in time for them to go up with ZERUBBABEL, as the latter must have left Babylon within a month after the decree was issued. When the liberation of the Hebrew captives was made known to them, coupled with the tidings that the vast body of their brethren had already departed with such haste for Jerusalem, they joyfully accepted the offer to return to their native Israel, although they were at first doubtful of what reception they would meet on their arrival.

*   *   *   *   *   *

Behold, when I come unto the children of Israel, and shall say unto them, The GOD of your fathers hath sent me unto you: and they shall say to me, What is his name ? what shall I say unto them ?

*   *   *   *   *   *

I AM THAT I AM: Thus shalt thou say unto the children of Israel, I AM hath sent me unto you.

Being assured that the same everlasting and eternal GOD, the I AM, who revealed himself to MOSES at the Burning Bush, and who brought forth their fathers out of Egypt with a mighty hand and an outstretched arm, would also sustain and defend them in the long and perilous journey across the desert or over the mountains, they hesitated no longer.   They at once turned their backs upon all the fascinations and luxuries of Babylon, and left the domes and spires of that idolatrous city, glistening in the sunlight behind them, as they resolutely started forth on their toilsome march.   With a sublime faith and an unselfish desire to honor the GOD of their fathers by rebuilding the temple to his Great and Sacred Name, they sought not to subserve their own ease and comfort; but, on the contrary, although their journey might be long, tedious and dreary, and their pathway rough, rugged and dangerous, yet they were determined to overcome every obstacle, endure every hardship, and brave every danger to promote that great and glorious work. What a lesson of faith, of unfeigned piety, of love to God, and of devotion and obedience to his service, does this little band of Hebrew captives, in a strange land, surrounded by all the allurements and temptations of an Eastern capital, set before us! How strikingly was that faith and devotion subsequently rewarded by the discovery of those inestimable treasures which gladdened their hearts, and which to-day thrill ours with an unspeakable joy!

Return of the Captives from Babylon to Jerusalem

There were two routes from Babylon to Jerusalem; one across the northern part of the Desert of Arabia, which was but little frequented; and the other up by the banks of the River Euphrates and around by the way of Tadmor and Damascus, and so down into Palestine by the plains of Jordan. The latter was, unquestionably, the route taken by the Chaldeans when returning with their captives from the destruction of Jerusalem, and such would naturally be the route of those returning from the captivity, as in this way they would avoid crossing an extensive desert which could supply neither water nor provisions.

*   *   *   *   *   *

LORD, I cry unto thee: make haste unto me: give ear unto my voice. Let my prayer be set forth before thee as incense, and the lifting up of my hands as the evening sacrifice. Set a

watch, O LORD, before my mouth; keep the
door of my lips. Incline not my heart to any
evil thing, to practice wicked works with men
that work iniquity. Let the righteous smite
me, it shall be a kindness; and let him reprove
me, it shall be an excellent oil. Mine eyes
are unto thee, O GOD the LORD; in thee is my
trust; leave not my soul destitute. Keep me
from the snare which they have laid for me,
and the gins of the workers of iniquity. Let
the wicked fall into their own nets, whilst that
I withal escape.

*   *   *   *   *   *

I cried unto the LORD with my voice; with
my voice unto the LORD did I make my supplication. I poured out my complaint before
him: I shewed before him my trouble. When
my spirit was overwhelmed within me, then
thou knewest my path. In the way wherein
I walked, have they privily laid a snare for me.
I looked on my right hand, and beheld, but
there was no man that would know me; refuge
failed me; no man cared for my soul. I cried
unto thee, O LORD: I said, thou art my refuge,
and my portion in the land of the living.

Attend unto my cry; for I am brought very
low: deliver me from my persecutors; for they
are stronger than I. Bring my soul out of
prison, that I may praise thy name.

*   *   *   *   *   *

Hear my prayer, O LORD, give ear to my
supplications; in thy faithfulness answer me,
and in thy righteousness. And enter not into
judgment with thy servant; for in thy sight
shall no man living be justified. For the
enemy hath persecuted my soul; he hath
smitten my life down to the ground; he hath
made me to dwell in darkness. Therefore is
my spirit overwhelmed within me; my heart
within me is desolate. Hear me speedily, O
LORD; my spirit faileth; hide not thy face from
me, lest I be like unto them that go down into
the pit. Cause me to hear thy loving-kindness
in the morning; for in thee do I trust; cause
me to know the way wherein I should walk;
for I lift up my soul unto thee. Teach me to
do thy will; for thou art my GOD; bring my
soul out of trouble, and of thy mercy cut off
my enemies, for I am thy servant.

THE UPPER ROUTE

THOSE who took the upper or northern route usually ascended on the eastern banks of the Euphrates, crossing that river in the vicinity of Circesium. Their course then lay up the west bank of the river, occasionally diverging from it, and then approaching it again, and, perhaps, following the winding of the bank for a considerable distance, until nearly opposite Palmyra or Tadmor, when it led in a westerly direction to that city, distant about twenty miles through the wilderness.

Palmyra, or "Tadmor, in the wilderness," was built by King SOLOMON, and was one of the most magnificent cities of the world. It was situated about one hundred miles east of Damascus, on a kind of oasis, separated from the habitable earth by a vast expanse of barren sands. Situated in the midst of this vast and arid plain, it was immediately surrounded by the most luxuriant vineyards, and beautiful groves of fig and palm trees, from the latter of which both its Hebrew and Greek names were derived.

Its situation was such as to draw to it, in its earlier days, the entire inland commerce between the great Persian empire on the East, and the countries lying on the Mediterranean Sea. Here the immense and richly-laden caravans from the East stopped and unloaded their treasures, which were exchanged for the commodities of the West; and hence it became not only a source of great revenue to SOLOMON, but was itself, perhaps, the richest city in the world. Its ruins are among the most famous monuments of past ages, and consist of almost countless remains of architectural splendor. In fact, it is now almost a forest of Corinthian pillars, erect and fallen. "In the space covered by these ruins," says a celebrated modern traveler, "we sometimes find a palace of which nothing remains but the court and the walls; sometimes a temple whose peristyle is half thrown down; and then a portico or gallery, or triumphal arch. Here stood groups of columns whose symmetry is destroyed by the fall of some of them; there we see them ranged in rows of such length that, like rows of trees, they deceive the sight, and assume the appearance of solid walls. And if we cast our eyes on the ground we behold nothing but subverted shafts, some above others, shattered to pieces or dislocated in their joints. And whichever way we look, the earth is strewed with vast stones half buried with broken entablatures, mutilated friezes, disfigured relics, effaced sculptures, violated tombs, and altars defiled with dust."

From Palmyra, the returning captives pursued their devious and rugged way to Damascus, and thence in a southerly direction over the mountainous ranges of Ancient Syria, Iturea, and Upper Israel, until they reached the plains of the Jordan, passing the famous clay-ground between Succoth and Zarthan, where the holy vessels for King SOLOMON's Temple were cast. Thus their weary and travel-worn feet again pressed the sacred soil of the Holy Land, and as they approached Jerusalem we can imagine with what mingled feelings of joy and sadness they beheld its ruins in the distance. Mournful, indeed, must have been their thoughts as they remembered the sack and destruction of their beauteous city—sad, indeed, must have been their memories of the captivity; and yet how their hearts must have swelled with pride and joy, as with the eye of faith they saw the city and temple of the LORD arise again, phœnix-like, from the ruin and desolation of Judah. With what alacrity must they have hastened over the brief distance still separating them from the longed-for Mount Moriah. They must have forgotten, in the inspiration of the scene, that they were weary, worn, and foot-sore; for now, although rough and rugged had been the road, long and toilsome their march, yet, sustained by a firm trust in the GREAT I AM, they had arrived at their journey's end.

*   *   *   *   *   *

Arrival at Jerusalem

The children of Israel, after their arrival at Jerusalem, erected a Tabernacle, similar in form to that of MOSES'.* Tradition, however, informs us that the Tabernacle of ZERUBBABEL differed from that of MOSES' in many particulars. The most holy place of

* Bishop Patrick. Commentaries on 1 Chron., ix. 11.

the original tabernacle contained the Ark of the Covenant, and the whole structure was designed wholly for the worship of GOD. That of ZERUBBABEL was used as a temporary place of worship, and the Sanctuary was also used for the meetings of the Grand Council, consisting of JOSHUA, ZERUBBABEL and HAGGAI. This tabernacle, according to the Masonic tradition, was divided into apartments by cross vails of blue, purple, scarlet, and white, at which guards were stationed.

Impostors among the Workmen

Sacred history relates that "When the adversaries of JUDAH and BENJAMIN heard that the children of the captivity builded the temple unto the LORD GOD of Israel; then they came to ZERUB-BABEL, and to the chief of the fathers, and said unto them, Let us build with you; for we seek your GOD, as ye do; and we do sacrifice unto him, since the days of ESAR-HADDON, King of Assur, which brought us up hither. But ZERUBBABEL and JOSHUA and the rest of the chief of the fathers of Israel said unto them, Ye have nothing to do with us to build an house unto our GOD; but we, ourselves together, will build unto the LORD GOD of Israel, as King CYRUS, the King of Persia hath commanded us."[*]

Masonic tradition asserts the same fact with more detail. From it we learn that no impostors from among these "adversaries," were permitted to engage in any part of the work, and, for this reason, the most scrupulous care was taken to ascertain the lineage of all the workmen. None were given employment unless they were able to trace their genealogy with certainty from those noble families of Giblimites who wrought so hard at the building of the first temple. These alone were permitted to engage in the great and glorious work of rebuilding the house of the LORD.

It is to be further remarked that among those who returned to labor on the second temple were many old men who had seen the glory of the first, and were present at its destruction by NEBU-ZARADAN, the lieutenant of the Chaldean monarch. This fact has been often doubted, but evidently without due consideration, for it is plainly asserted in Scripture.[*] In this connection, it must be remembered that the seventy years of captivity began from the fourth year of JEHOIACHIM, and that only fifty-two years intervened between the destruction of the temple and the return of ZERUB-

* Ezra, iv. 1-3.   † Ezra, iii. 12, and Haggai, ii. 3.

BABEL. If a Most Excellent Master had been twenty-three years of age when King SOLOMON's temple was destroyed, he would have been only seventy-five years old when the Hebrew captives reached Jerusalem. This view of the subject at once relieves the statement of all apparent inconsistency, and makes the matter plain to our comprehension.

♪♪ ♪♪ ♪♪

BLUE is emblematic of universal friendship and benevolence, and teaches us that those virtues should be as expansive in the breast of every Mason as the blue vault of heaven itself.

And MOSES answered and said, But, behold, they will not believe me, nor hearken unto my voice: for they will say, The LORD hath not appeared unto thee. And the LORD said unto him, What is that in thine hand? And he said, A rod. And he said, Cast it on the ground. And he cast it on the ground, and it became a serpent; and MOSES fled from before it. And the LORD said unto MOSES, Put forth thine hand, and take it by the tail. And he put forth his hand, and caught it, and it became a rod in his hand. That they may believe that the LORD GOD of their fathers, the GOD of ABRAHAM, the GOD of ISAAC, and the GOD of JACOB hath appeared unto thee.

The serpent is a symbol of frequent use in all the various rites, though of not so general use in the York rite as in the others.

Much speculation has been indulged in as to the miracle of MOSES' Rod; and many strange and fabulous traditions are given by OLIVER and other writers.

The rod of MOSES was undoubtedly the ordinary pastoral staff or crook of the shepherd, which he was using while tending the flocks of JETHRO, and all its efficacy and superiority was due alone to the divine power of GOD.

The symbol of the serpent may naturally be employed to remind us of the fall of the race in ADAM by the wiles of the tempter, and of the promised restoration of the race by the bruising of the serpent's head by the seed of the woman. *It thus alludes to the loss and recovery.*

The Ark of Safety

The first ark, or, as it is commonly called, the ark of NOAH, was constructed by SHEM, HAM, and JAPHET, under the direction of NOAH, and in obedience to the command of GOD.

♫ ♫ ♫ ♩

PURPLE, being formed of a due admixture of blue and scarlet, is intended to remind us of the intimate connection which exists between symbolic Masonry and the Royal Arch degrees.

And the LORD said furthermore unto him, Put now thy hand into thy bosom. And he put his hand into his bosom; and when he took it out, behold, his hand was leprous as snow. And he said, Put thine hand into thy bosom again. And he put his hand into his bosom again; and plucked it out of his bosom, and, behold, it was turned again as his other flesh. And it shall come to pass, if they will not believe thee,

neither hearken to the voice of the firs
that they will believe the voice of the latter sign.

The leprous hand is another of those symbols employed in the
rituals of Masonry which refer to a loss and a recovery. Leprosy
was a loathsome disease of the skin and tissues, and was regarded
by the Jews and other ancient nations as a judgment from the hand
of GOD; and was, therefore, believed to be entirely incurable except
by miraculous power. The restoration of the leprous hand to
health was, therefore, a striking symbol of the Divine Presence
with MOSES, and serves to assure the neophyte in search after truth
that the Deity will reward his earnest labors.

The Ark of Alliance

The second ark, or ark of alliance, was constructed by MOSES,
AHOLIAB, and BEZALEEL, in accordance with a pattern given by
GOD. It was the first constructed, as it was the first in importance,
of all the furniture of the original tabernacle. Its chief use seems
to have been to contain, inviolate, the Divine autograph of the
two tables, and to serve as the visible seat of the Divine Presence.
It was also a pledge to the people of Israel of the solemn covenant
which GOD had made with his chosen servants.

♫ ♫ ♫ ♪

SCARLET is emblematic of that fervency and zeal which
should actuate all Royal Arch Masons, and is peculiarly
characteristic of this degree.

And it shall come to pass, if they will not
believe also these two signs, neither hearken
unto thy voice, that thou shalt take of the water
of the river, and pour it upon the dry land: and
the water which thou takest out of the river
shall become blood upon the dry land.

The symbol of the water turned to blood, like the others we have considered, has also a reference to a loss and a recovery; a transition from ignorance to knowledge, from darkness to light, from death to life. Its appropriateness in the lessons of a degree like the Royal Arch will be readily seen and understood by all those who have studied the teachings of our sublime ritual.

The Ark of Imitation

Here, too, we have an allusion to the third ark, which fills so important a place among the relics and symbols of the higher degrees of Freemasonry; and concerning which the Fraternity possess so many interesting traditions. It was an exact copy of the Ark of the Covenant, and, after its recovery, was placed in the sanctuary of the new tabernacle by JOSHUA, ZERUBBABEL, and HAGGAI.

The Signet of Truth

It is impossible to ascertain the precise form of the signet of ZERUBBABEL, or the inscription thereon; although some ingenious writers have attempted to do so. Some have supposed it to have been a triangular plate; but the most reasonable conjecture is, that it was a ring on which was engraved an equilateral triangle with the Hebrew letter *yod* in the center.

The use of the signet ring was almost universal among the Jews and other ancient nations, and frequent references to them are found in Scripture. When a king intrusted his signet to a person, it conferred on that person the authority and sanction of the monarch, and was the usual mode employed to authenticate a delegated power. The symbolical use of the signet of ZERUBBABEL is to invest the aspirant after truth with a token which shall enable him to prosecute his search, and also serve as a pledge of his ultimate victory, if he perseveres.

♪ ♪ ♪ ♪

WHITE is emblematic of that purity of life and rectitude of conduct, by which alone we can expect to gain admission into the Holy of Holies above.

Incense burns upon our holy altar both day and night.

In the seventh month, in the one and twentieth day of the month, came the word of the LORD by the prophet HAGGAI, saying,

Speak now to ZERUBBABEL, the son of SHEALTIEL, governor of Judah, and to JOSHUA, the son of JOSEDECH, the High-Priest, and to the residue of the people, saying, Who is left among you that saw this house in her glory? and how do ye see it now? is it not in your eyes, in comparison of it, as nothing? Yet now be strong, O ZERUBBABEL, and be strong, O JOSHUA,

son of JOSEDECH the High-Priest: and be strong,
all ye people of the land, saith the LORD, and
work: for I am with you, saith the LORD of
hosts: according to the word that I covenanted
with you when ye came out of Egypt, so my
spirit remaineth among you: fear ye not.   For
thus saith the LORD of hosts, Yet once, it is a
little while, and I will shake the heavens, and
the earth, and the sea, and the dry land; and I
will shake all nations, and the desire of all
nations shall come, and I will fill this house with
glory.   The silver is mine, and the gold is mine.
*The glory of this latter house shall be greater than
of the former*, and in this place will I give peace.

In that day will I take thee, O ZERUBBABEL,
my servant, the son of SHEALTIEL, saith the
LORD, and will make thee as a Signet: for I
have chosen thee.

*   *   *   *   *   *

None but those faithful craftsmen who have received the signet
of Truth can be admitted to participate in building the second
temple of "Holiness to the LORD"—and for that reason it is absolutely necessary that every neophyte in Masonic science should
give evidence of his proficiency in the sublime principles of the
art, and of his ability to engage in the important work.   Being
satisfied on so vital a point, it is proper that his attention should
be called to his symbolical working tools, and that he should be
taught how to use them in a proper manner.

The WORKING TOOLS of a Royal Arch Mason may be here explained.

The Working Tools of a Royal Arch Mason are the *Crow, Pickax,* and *Spade.* The *Crow* is used by operative Masons to raise things of great weight and bulk; the *Pickax* to loosen the soil, and prepare it for digging; and the *Spade* to remove rubbish. But the Royal Arch Mason is emblematically taught to use them for more noble purposes. By them he is reminded that it is his sacred duty to lift from his mind the heavy weight of passions and prejudices which encumber his progress toward virtue, loosening the hold which long habits of sin and folly have had upon his disposition, and removing the rubbish of vice and ignorance, which prevents him from beholding that eternal foundation of truth and wisdom upon which he is to erect the spiritual and moral temple of his second life.

*   *   *   *   *   *

The industrious student of our mysteries cannot fail to draw from these simple tools still further food for moral reflections. To such an one the *crow* will be a striking emblem of uprightness of life, integrity of character, and unyielding discharge of duty; the sound of the *pickax* will remind him of the sound of the last trumpet, when the grave shall give up its dead; and the *spade* will depict to his mind the grave itself into which the mortal part of man is laid away from sight.

The Royal Arch Mason cannot fail to learn further from the diligent use of these implements, that he must search to the very foundations which underlie all human knowledge if he would find that great object of all his earthly pilgrimage—the end of his labors. Truth may be buried for a time under a cumbrous mass of error; the ruins of a better civilization may have been thrown down upon it; its very existence may be forgotten, but the diligent seeker after it will surely find it.

> "Truth crushed to earth shall rise again,
> Th' eternal years of GoD are hers."

*   *   *   *   *   *

*   *   *   *   *   *

This is the word of the LORD unto ZERUBBA-BEL, saying, Not by might nor power, but by my spirit. Who art thou, O great mountain? Before ZERUBBABEL thou shalt become a plain, and he shall bring forth the head-stone thereof with shouting, crying, Grace, grace unto it. Moreover, the word of the LORD came unto me, saying, The hands of ZERUBBABEL have laid the foundation of this house; his hands shall also finish it; and thou shalt know that the LORD of hosts hath sent me unto you. For who hath·

despised the day of small things? for they shall
rejoice, and shall see the plummet in the hand of
ZERUBBABEL, with those seven.—ZACH. iv. 6-10.

*   *   *   *   *   *

In our remarks on a preceding degree, we have shown that arches
and key-stones were known and employed in the construction of
the temple; and it only remains to say that recent discoveries
have been made of arched passages and vaults under the ancient
foundations of the temple, which were undoubtedly constructed at
the time when King SOLOMON laid those foundations. In BART-
LETT's "Walks about the city of Jerusalem" (p. 170) is described
one of these arched vaults under that part of the Mosque of OMAR,
which occupies the site of the Sanctum Sanctorum of the ancient
temple.

*   *   *   *   *   *

In that day will I raise up the tabernacle of
DAVID that is fallen, and close up the breaches
thereof; and I will raise up his ruins, and I will
build it as in the days of old.—AMOS ix. 11.

The Ark of the Covenant

What became of the Ark at the destruction of the temple is a question much debated among the Rabbins; but it is agreed on all hands that it was not taken to Babylon with the holy vessels. Some of the Jewish writers contend that it was taken and hidden in a rock by the prophet JEREMIAH, who then sealed up this rock with his finger, writing thereon the name of GOD.* "Others assert that King JOSIAH, being foretold by HULDAH, the prophetess, that the temple would speedily after his death be destroyed, caused the ark to be put in a vault under ground, which SOLOMON, foreseeing this destruction, had caused of purpose to be built for the preserving of it."†

* 2 Maccabees, ii. 1-7.   † Prideaux. Con., vol. i., p. 247.

The most learned commentators are of the opinion that it was destroyed with the temple. Such is the Masonic tradition, and there are many circumstances to confirm its truth. It is certain it was not in the second temple; and Dr. LIGHTFOOT,* Dean PRIDEAUX,† and others assert that an exact imitation or copy of the original ark was substituted for it in the ceremonials of the second temple. Of this imitation, and of its origin and construction, we unhesitatingly assert that the traditions of Masonry give the only authentic account. And here, too, we have another symbolical allusion to a loss and a recovery.

This imitation or second ark possessed none of the prerogatives and honors with which the first ark was invested by GOD's own appointment. There was no cloud of glory over it, and no oracles were given from it. It was only a representative or type of the original, which was itself but a type of the Messiah.

*   *   *   *   *   *

In the beginning GOD created the heaven and the earth. And the earth was without form, and void; and darkness was upon the face of the deep; and the Spirit of GOD moved upon the face of the waters. And GOD said, Let there be light; and there was light.

* Lightfoot. Pros. of the Temple, c. xv., § 4.
† Prideaux. Con., vol. i., p. 243.

And it came to pass, when MOSES had made an end of writing the words of this law in a book, until they were finished, that MOSES commanded the Levites which bare the ark of the covenant of the LORD, saying, Take this Book of the Law, and put it in the side of the ark of the covenant of the LORD your GOD, that it may be there for a witness against thee.

And thou shalt put the mercy-seat above, upon the ark: and in the ark thou shalt put the testimony that I shall give thee.

And MOSES said, This is the thing which the LORD commandeth, Fill an omer of the manna, to be kept for your generations; that they may see the bread wherewith I have fed you in the wilderness, when I brought you forth from the land of Egypt.   And MOSES said unto AARON, Take a pot, and put an omer full of manna therein, and lay it up before the LORD, to be kept for your generations.   As the LORD commanded MOSES, so AARON laid it up before the testimony to be kept.

And the LORD said unto MOSES, Bring AARON'S rod again before the testimony, to be kept for a token.

*   *   *   *   *   *

The Pot of Manna

The manna was a small, round thing, as small as the hoar-frost on the ground. It is described in Scripture as being like coriander seed, white, and the taste of it like wafers made with honey.* The name is supposed by scholars to be derived from the two words: *mân hu, what is this?* For forty years this article was miraculously supplied to the Israelites, while sojourning in the wilderness, it having ceased while they were encamped at Gilgal, immediately after they had celebrated the passover for the first time in the promised land. Three distinct miracles accompanied the gift of manna, all wrought in attestation of the sanctity of the Sabbath; and which, in this connection, serve to remind the Mason of those early instructions which he received as a Fellow-Craft and Mark Master. These miracles were as follows: 1. A double quantity was supplied on the sixth day; 2. On the Sabbath, or seventh day, none was furnished; 3. That which was kept from the sixth to the seventh day was good and sweet, while that which was kept from any other day to the next day bred worms and became offensive. To commemorate this long-continued and wonderful miracle, Moses was instructed that a *golden pot†* should be provided, and that an omer or one man's portion of the manna should be put therein, and be laid up in the side of the ark. There it was to remain for their generations so long as the ark itself existed, as a memorial of the miraculous manner in which the children of Israel were supplied with that article of food for forty years in the wilderness. This pot is depicted on Samaritan medals in the form of an urn, with a lid or cover. The Rabbins considered the manna to be a type of the Jewish Messiah, who was to be the spiritual food of his people. It masonically teaches us that as the Israelites fed on manna from heaven, so should we spiritually feed on that *Truth* which is the great object of our investigations.

* Exodus, xvi., 31.   † Hebrews, ix., 4.

Aaron's Rod

A signal attestation was granted by GOD to AARON'S official authority. Twelve rods or branches of the almond tree were taken, one for the head of each house or tribe of Israel; and upon the rod of the tribe of LEVI was written the name of AARON. The rods were laid together in the tabernacle of the congregation before the testimony; and the next day when MOSES went into the tabernacle, the rod which had AARON'S name upon it "was budded, and brought forth buds, and bloomed blossoms, and yielded almonds." This wonderful miracle was made known to the people by an exhibition of the rod; but it was immediately taken back into the tabernacle, by divine command, to be kept there "for a token against the rebels," and also as a testimony of the appointment of the Levites to the priesthood.

The Book of the Law

"There was a tradition among the Jews," says Dr. MACKEY, "that the Book of the Law was lost during the captivity, and that it was among the treasures discovered during the building of the second temple." Dean PRIDEAUX, to the same effect, says that "Many of the ancient fathers hold that all the Scriptures were lost and destroyed in the Babylonish captivity, and that EZRA restored them all again by divine revelation. Thus saith IRENAEUS, and thus say TURTULLIAN, CLEMENS ALEXANDRINUS, BASIL, and others."*

Most commentators, however, reject the tradition, and assert that EZRA did no more than to collect as many copies of the sacred writings as he could, and out of them all set forth a correct edition; and this appears to be the opinion of Dr. PRIDEAUX himself.

*Prideaux, Con., vol. i., p. 432.

The Scriptures were originally written in the old Hebrew or Samaritan character, and copies of them were also made in that character until the captivity.* During the captivity the Hebrews, to a great extent, lost the use of that language, and hence EZRA transcribed the law into the Chaldaic character, in order that it might be generally understood by the people. This was the origin of the Chaldaic paraphrases as they were called.† EZRA also introduced synagogues among the Jews, and by himself and his scribes multiplied copies of the Scriptures and caused them to be read in the synagogues that he established.‡

It is, however, a generally conceded fact that twice in the Jewish history there were no copies of the Scriptures known to be in existence. It is apparent that the Book of the Law was very rare in the reign of JEHOSHAPHAT, because we are told that when he sent teachers through all Judah to instruct the people in the law of GOD, they carried with them "The Book of the Law of the LORD,"§ which, as PRIDEAUX remarks, they would not have done, had there been any copies of the law in the cities to which they went. In the succeeding years, during the wicked reign of MANASSEH and his successor, it is evident that no copy of the Book of the Law was known to exist; for when HILKIAH found the law in the temple,‖ neither he nor King JOSIAH would have been so surprised at it, had copies of it been common. Their conduct on that occasion sufficiently proves that neither of them had ever seen the book before. This opinion is now held by most commentators, as well as by the early fathers,¶ who assert that all the copies known to have been in existence were destroyed by the injunctions of MANASSEH and AMNON, his son and successor. The only copies that escaped destruction were those which were preserved by the conservators of Jewish Masonry.

It is probable that HILKIAH and JOSIAH took care that this copy of the law, found by them, should be laid up in the ark from whence it had been taken, to preserve it from destruction at the hands of MANASSEH; and there are some reasons for supposing that partial copies of it may have been made, which were preserved among the captives in Babylon; but the Scriptures are silent upon the subject.

---

* Prideaux, Con., vol. ii., p. 58. Dr. Wm. Smith's Dictionary of the Bible.

† Union Bible Dictionary. ‡ Prideaux, Con., vol. 2, p. 13.

§ 2 Chronicles, xvii., 9. ‖ 2 Kings, xxii., and 2 Chronicles, xxxiv.

¶ Dr. Oliver, Hist. Landmarks, vol. ii., p. 272. Dr. Prideaux, Con., vol. i., p. 137.

A Jewish tradition, however, relates that the prophetess HULDAH, foreseeing the destruction of the temple, took this Book of the Law, and hid it in the temple. But whatever may have been its temporary disposition, it is generally agreed by scholars that the book perished in the temple, and that thus the only known complete copy of the law was again destroyed. In fact, KENNICOTT asserts that this was the original Pentateuch of MOSES, in which opinion he is probably correct.

The Jews have a tradition that at the rebuilding of the temple, by ZERUBBABEL, another complete copy of the "Book of the Law" was found hidden in a part of the temple which had not been destroyed.*

The Masonic traditions not only assert this to be the fact, but give such minute details of the circumstances attending the deposit and preservation of this book, as well as so circumstantial an account of the place, time, and mode of its discovery, that they certainly seem to be true. If these traditions are rejected, the student is left environed with such difficulties that, to escape them, some have supposed that EZRA was inspired by GOD to rewrite the Scriptures anew, the old copies being all destroyed.† But, on the other hand, if the truth of the Masonic traditions on this subject be admitted, they at once rationally account for the preservation and recovery of the Book of the Law, long lost, yet afterward found; and this, too, in a way entirely consistent with the few historical facts which appear in this connection in the sacred writings, and equally so with the genius of the Jewish religion and customs. The claim, therefore, that Freemasonry has preserved the only authentic account of the manner in which GOD's blessed Book of the Law was preserved to mankind, is not so chimerical as many persons have supposed. Indeed, any person who has given this subject the attention it demands cannot fail to admit the force which all the circumstances give to the Masonic position on this subject. It remains only to answer a single objection which has been urged against the truth of the tradition. It is said that the writing would have lost its legibility in so long a time as four hundred and seventy years, and hence the whole claim must be fabulous. It is sufficient to answer, in the light of modern discoveries, that the writings of the Egyptians have been frequently found in connection with mummies, which are conceded to be at least three thousand years old, and yet remained perfectly legible. Modern discoveries in science, history, and the antiquities of the eastern nations have invariably sustained and confirmed the traditions of Masonry, and so, in like manner, this objection we are considering melts away before the light of modern research and investigation, as all other objections against the Order will, when brought to that test.

To the wisdom and foresight of SOLOMON we may then reasonably ascribe the preservation of the Book of the Law; and to the zealous descendants of the ancient Giblimites we may justly ascribe its recovery; and, finally, in the carefully guarded traditions of our glorious old Institution may be found the only reasonable and satisfactory account of those events, fraught with such stupendous results to our race—which is the summit of the glory of the Order.

*　　*　　*　　*　　*　　*

And GOD spake unto MOSES, and said unto him, I am the LORD; and I appeared unto ABRAHAM, unto ISAAC, and unto JACOB, by the name of GOD ALMIGHTY; but by my name JEHOVAH was I not known to them.

The Tetragrammaton

יהוה

The Ineffable Word or Tetragrammaton* is, perhaps, the most generally diffused symbol to be found in the ancient rites and mysteries, for there is probably no system of initiation in which it does not appear in some form.

It is composed of the past, present, and future tense of the Hebrew verb הָיָה *to be;* signifying was, is, and shall be.† It is

* So called from the two Greek words *tetra*, four, and *gramma*, letter; and hence the term signifies *the four lettered word.* It is applied only to the Hebrew name of Deity, not being used in connection with other words.

† It is a singular fact that the verb "*to be*" in most, if not all, languages, is irregular in its construction and conjugation. This verb is also used in all languages as an auxiliary to be added to the other verbs to assist in their conjugation. Putting these facts together, we have then embodied, and implied

also composed of three syllables, a sacred number, symbolical of form, stability and power. Three lines are necessary to form a figure, three columns at least are necessary for firm self-support, and *tres faciunt leges** is an ancient legal maxim. The Jewish Rabbins affirm that the letters composing it abound in mysteries, and some of them assert that "he who pronounces it shakes heaven and earth, and inspires the very angels with terror." "A sovereign authority resides in it; it governs the world; it is the fountain of all grace and blessings, the channel through which GOD's mercies are conveyed to men." JOSEPHUS calls it "the shuddering name of GOD." It was also called by the Jews the unutterable or incommunicable name. It is usually marked or denoted in Jewish books by the initial letter alone, the Hebrew י *yod*, and was frequently written in Samaritan characters, in place of the Hebrew, lest strangers should discover and profane it. It was held in such veneration and awe by the Israelites that they never pronounced it, always substituting for it, when reading, the word *Adonai*, LORD.

This sacred word is supposed to have been known by the antedeluvian patriarchs down to and including ENOCH, when it was lost. It was specially communicated to MOSES at the Burning Bush, by the LORD himself, as his most sacred appellation, to be reverenced by his chosen people. When MOSES asked to know in whose name he was to demand the liberation of the Hebrews from the thraldom of PHARAOH, the Almighty revealed to him this great Name in these majestic and sublime words: "Thus shalt thou say unto the children of Israel, JEHOVAH, the GOD of your fathers, the GOD of ABRAHAM, the GOD of ISAAC, and the GOD of JACOB hath sent me unto you; this is my name forever, and this is my memorial unto all generations."* Afterward, when the efforts of MOSES to obtain

in the Tetragrammaton, these three distinct ideas: First, the eternity of God, as embracing in himself the past, present, and future of existence; second, the mystery of that existence and attributes, and the unsearchable ways of his Providence, denoted by the irregularity of the verb from which his name is derived; and, lastly, the omnipotent power of the Deity, indicated in the auxiliary use of that same verb.

* "Three make laws."

* Exodus, iii., 15. It will be observed that whenever the Hebrew Tetragrammaton, יהוה *Jehovah*, occurs, our version follows the Jewish custom, and almost always translates it LORD or GOD; but in all such cases the word substituted is printed in small capitals, to show that it in reality stands for Jehovah. Our version, therefore, fails to convey the full import of the original text, unless this fact is borne in mind.

their release, only increased the burdens and tasks of the Hebrews, and he repented that he had been sent on his mission to his countrymen, the LORD again, and in still more emphatic language, declared the Tetragrammaton to be his peculiar name, when he said: "I am JEHOVAH; and I appeared unto ABRAHAM, unto ISAAC, and unto JACOB by the name of GOD ALMIGHTY, but by my name, JEHOVAH, was I not known to them."* We are here explicitly told that GOD's true name is יהוה, but that he was known to the three patriarchs only by the name of *El Shaddai.* Thus solemnly promulgated to MOSES by the Almighty, the Tetragrammaton at once became invested with a peculiar awe among the children of Israel, which was in after years very much increased by the general belief that the terms of the third commandment forbade the use of this sacred Name, except by the High-Priest, on the day of expiation. Even to this day no pious Jew will speak the word, but whenever he meets with it in Scripture he substitutes for it *Adonai.*

The use of the word being thus abandoned, its true pronunciation was lost, for the reason that the letters of the Hebrew language can give no possible indication of the correct pronunciation of any word to a person who has never heard the word spoken. The Hebrew alphabet consisted entirely of consonants, hence the vowels were sounded, but not written. Thus the Tetragrammaton was written with four consonants, י *yod,* pronounced yŏth; ה *he,* hay; ו *vau,* vwauv; and ה *he,* hay; making, when combined, יהוה, or, as nearly as we can represent it in English, yhvh or Jhvh. A person who had never heard those letters pronounced, of course, would never be able to tell how they were to be sounded. Yet a Hebrew that had been taught orally the true pronunciation of the words composing his language had no more difficulty in speaking them correctly than we have in knowing that when we meet Dr. it should be pronounced Doctor, or that Geo. stands for George.† From this view of the Hebrew language it will be

* Exodus, vi., 2, 3.

† The Hebrew language continued to be written in this manner without vowels until about the time of the Christian era, when the Masoretic or vowel points were invented. The date of this invention is variously stated by scholars, some contending that they were introduced soon after the Babylonish captivity; others asserting that it was the work of the Masorites just before the birth of Christ; and still others, that the system was not perfected until after the completion of the Talmuds, five hundred years after Christ. For the several

apparent that the only way in which an Israelite could understand
the true pronunciation of any Hebrew word was by hearing it
spoken; and hence, when the Tetragrammaton ceased to be spoken,
Adonai being always substituted for it, in a short time its true pronunciation would necessarily have been forgotten and entirely lost.

The true pronunciation of the great and sacred Name was preserved
by the High-Priests, each one of whom received it from his predecessor, and retained its correct sound by uttering it aloud three
times, once a year on the day of atonement, when he entered the
Holy of Holies of the tabernacle or temple.   The traditions of
Masonry relate that King SOLOMON was also in possession of the
true pronunciation of the Tetragrammaton, and that he communicated it to his colleagues at the building of his temple.   It was
believed by the Jews that the power and wisdom of SOLOMON arose
from his possession of the Ineffable Name, and that by it he was
enabled to erect the temple itself.

We pronounce the Tetragrammaton, *Jehovah;* but what are the
correct vowel sounds to be supplied is a vexed question, among
Hebrew scholars, which will never perhaps be definitely settled.
In the degrees of the Ancient and Accepted rite, many traditions
are preserved, which explain the mysteries connected with the
Ineffable Word, and the different pronunciations which have been
at different periods applied to it are explained.   Among these are
the following Javh, Jao, Jaoth, Java, Juba, Jaa, Jah, Jehovah,
Juha, Jeva, Jova, Jevo, Jevah, Johe.

The true pronunciation, however chimerical it may appear, is
said to be preserved in the ritual of Freemasonry, and, as we
have before remarked, is the grand symbol of the Order.   It
was corrupted among all the heathen nations, in the rites of whom
it yet maintained a prominent place.   Thus among the Syriac
nations we find it contracted into a biliteral word JAH.   Among
the Chaldeans we find it changed to BEL, or *Belus,* or *Baal.*   Among
the Egyptians we find it changed to ON, derived, perhaps, from the
Hindoo AUM or OM.   Among the Latins we find *Jupiter* and *Jove.*

From what has been said, it will be seen that the Tetragrammaton was the Word of Words among the Jews, or, as it has been
sometimes called, the KING NAME.   In Scripture, Truth or Light
is frequently used as its synonym.   It is the *Logos* of the ancients,

arguments in favor of these views, the reader is referred to Prideaux, Con..
vol. i., p. 450, and the different Hebrew grammars.

No single word in our language can express its pregnant meaning, embracing, as it does, not only the *Word*, as a word, a written or vocal symbol of an idea, but also the sentient creative Power, which conceives and expresses it. In this sense it is used in the Scriptures and translated "the Word." "In the beginning was the Word, and the Word was with GOD, and the Word was GOD." Finally, the contemplation of the history and character of the great, mysterious and sacred name of Deity cannot but fill us with fear and trembling, and lead us with admiration to view the glorious works of creation, to adore their great Creator, to esteem him the chief good, to implore his blessing upon all laudable undertakings, to trust in and lean upon him in every hour of trial and danger, and to never mention his name but with that reverential awe which is so justly due from a creature to its Creator.

The key has been used as a symbol from very remote ages. The Egyptians employed it as the symbol of Anubis, the dog-star, because they conceived that at the rising of that star the old year was closed and a new one was commenced. From this, the use of the symbol was extended to the opening and closing the place of departed spirits. At an early period it came to be used as a symbol of power, and in modern times we note this use of the key in transferring the power and authority over a city, or in giving possession of a building. It is also a symbol of secrecy, and may appropriately impress upon the mind of the initiate the importance of safely locking within his own breast those valuable truths which, amid the most bitter persecutions, have been transmitted from generation to generation, for the benefit of the true Sons of Light.

Its principal use, however, is to teach us that the Book of the Law furnishes the only key with which to unlock the deep hidden mysteries of our science, while a correct knowledge of our mysteries in turn solves many difficult things in the Book of the Law itself, or in other words that Freemasonry is the handmaid of Religion.

THE SHEKINAH AND THE BATHKOLL

AMONG those things which were wanting in the second temple, and which constituted the main glory of the first, there are three which deserve especial attention, viz: the Ark of the Covenant with the mercy-seat; the Shekinah or Divine presence, and the Bathkoll. A substitute was found for the original Ark, as we have seen; but this possessed none of the glories of the first. The Shekinah, which was a token of GOD'S presence among his people, "was a very shining flame or amazing splendor of light, enveloped in a visible cloud,"* resting over the mercy-seat on the Ark. It first appeared when MOSES consecrated the Tabernacle, and was afterward transferred to the temple at the solemn dedication of that edifice by King SOLOMON. It continued to rest upon the Ark in the same visible manner until the destruction of the temple.†

It never appeared again until it was temporarily renewed by GOD to punish the impious attempt of JULIAN, the Apostate, to frustrate the prophecy of CHRIST, by rebuilding the temple after its final destruction by TITUS.

The Bathkoll, a compound Hebrew word, signifying the daughter voice, or the daughter of a voice, was a term applied to a voice from Heaven. It was used to denote particularly the oracular voice delivered from the mercy-seat, when GOD was consulted there by the High-Priest.

The sacred Ark of the first temple being indeed lost, it was very naturally supposed, by those who had seen that edifice in its splendor, that the Shekinah and the Bathkoll had departed from Judah forever. The "ancient men" wept with a loud voice, believing that the former glory would never be fully restored to Jerusalem until the Messiah should appear as the true Shekinah and Bathkoll, the Divine presence and Oracle, among mankind.

The Grand Council, without doubt, took measures to preserve, with the most religious care, the sacred treasures so miraculously restored to them, and for that purpose, tradition states, suitable persons were exalted to the high honor of guarding them from loss or profanation.

*   *   *   *   *   *

* Bishop Patrick.   † Prideaux, Con., vol. i., p. 247.

An interesting annunciation is now made with grateful thanks to God for the discovery, when the following ode should be sung, the companions all standing:

ROYAL ARCH ODE

Music—*Nuremberg*

Joy, the sa - cred law is found,

Now the tem - ple stands com - plete,

Glad - ly let us gath - er round,

Where the pon - tiff holds his seat;

Now he spreads the vol - ume wide,

Open - ing forth its leaves to day,

And the mon - arch by his side,

Ga - zes on this bright dis - play,

Joy, the secret *vault* is found;
　　Full the sunbeam falls within,
Pointing darkly under ground
　　To the treasure we would win.
They have brought it forth to light,
　　And again it cheers the earth;
All its leaves are purely bright,
　　Shining in their newest worth.

This shall be the sacred *mark*
　Which shall guide us to the skies;
Bearing, like a *holy ark*,
　All the hearts who love to rise;
This shall be the *corner-stone*
　Which the builders threw away,
But was found the only one
　Fitted for the *arch's* stay.

This shall be the *gavel* true
　At whose sound the crowd shall bend,
Giving to the *law* its due;
　This shall be the faithful friend;
This the token which shall bring
　Kindness to the sick and poor,
Hastening on, on angel's wing,
　To the lone and *darksome door*.

This shall crown the mighty *arch*,
　When the temple springs on high,
And the brethren bend their march,
　Wafting *incense* to the sky.
Then the solemn strain shall swell
　From the bosom and the tongue,
And the Master's glory tell
　In the harmony of song.

Here the exile, o'er the waste,
　Trudging homeward, shall repose;
All his toils and dangers past,
　Here his long sojournings close.
Entering through the sacred *vails*,
　To the holy cell he bends;
Then, as sinking nature fails,
　Hope in glad fruition ends.

*   *   *   *   *   *

The High-Priest will then invest the candidates with important secrets of the degree, which should always be accompanied with an explanatory

LECTURE

*   *   *   *   *   *

The name is expressive of self-existence and eternity, and is applicable only to that great being who was, is, and shall be; to him who created all things, to him whose hands are open to supply our every want, and to him alone who is the source of every Mason's hope. It is considered by Masons as the symbol of Truth. It is the perfection of Divine Truth, which every good Mason is seeking to advance, whether it be by the aid of the theological ladder, or passing between the pillars of strength and establishment, or wandering in darkness,

*   *   *   *   *   *

beset on every side with dangers, or traveling over rough and rugged roads, weary and worn—whatever be the direction of our journey, or how accomplished, light and truth are the ultimate objects of our search and our labor.

* * * * * *

THE WORKING-TOOLS,

In addition to the *Crow*, *Pickax*, and *Spade*, whose use you have already learned, are the *Square* and *Compass*, which have been presented to your view in every degree of Masonry through which you have passed.

The *Square* teaches us, as Royal Arch Masons, that GOD has made all things square, upright, and perfect. The *Compass* is an instrument used by operative Masons to describe circles, every part of the circumference of which is equally near and equally distant from the center. The circle is, therefore, a striking emblem of the relation in which the creature stands to his Creator. As every part of the circumference of a circle is equally near and equally distant from its center, so is every creature whom GOD has made to him equally near and equally distant.

THE EQUILATERAL OR PERFECT TRIANGLE,

*   *   *   *

Is emblematical of the three essential attributes of Deity— namely, Omnipresence, Omniscience, and Omnipotence; and as the three equal angles form but one TRIANGLE, so these three equal attributes constitute but one GOD,

*   *   *   *   *   *

This emblem was adopted by the ancients as a symbol of the Deity—as embracing in himself the three stages of time—the Past, the Present, and the Future. Among the Hebrews a yod, or point in the center of an equilateral triangle, was one of the modes of expressing the incommunicable name of JEHOVAH. For this reason, the number THREE has always been held in high estimation by the Fraternity. We find it pervading the whole ritual. There are three degrees of Ancient Craft Masonry, three principal officers of a Lodge, three supports, three ornaments, three greater and three lesser lights, three movable and three immovable jewels, three principal tenets, three rounds of JACOB's ladder, three working-tools of a Fellow-Craft, three principal orders of architecture, three important human senses, three ancient Grand Masters, etc.

*　　*　　*　　*　　*　　*

In short, the allusion to the triangle may be found wherever we turn our steps in Freemasonry. It is held in still higher estimation by all Royal Arch Masons. There are three principal officers who compose the Grand Council, three Grand Masters of the Vails, three—and only three—can be exalted at the same time.

*　　*　　*　　*　　*　　*

Our altar is triangular, our jewels are triangular, and our

*　　*　　*　　*　　*　　*

The Number Three

The frequent recurrence of this number in the ancient mythologies, in the Bible histories, and in the Ritual of Masonry, is almost incredible to a person who has never examined the subject. Instances of its use can be multiplied until the mind grows weary. The following are given as examples rather than as any attempt to exhaust the subject. Among the ancient references to this number we find the following: Oracles were delivered from a tripod; libations were threefold; there were supposed to be three worlds;

the magical rod of the Hierophants had three heads of silver; if any revealed the mysteries they were told they would die in three days; and in the celebration of the mysteries the Hierophant smote the coffin three times with his tripartite rod. The Greeks divided their gods into three kinds; and DEMOCRITUS wrote a book called "Trilogenia," in which he endeavored to prove that all things sprang from the number three. Among the Druids the number three was held in the highest veneration, and was one of their most sacred symbols, and hence their use of the mistletoe and shamrock, because their leaves were tripartite. Of them a writer says: "They turn three times round their karns; round the persons they bless three times; three turns they make round St. BARR's church, and three times round the well."

The number three was a symbol of marriage, friendship, and peace, because it was said to unite contraries; it was also an emblem of wisdom and prudence, because men are said to order the present, foresee the future, and learn experience from the past. Its influence was said to extend to all nature, embracing the birth, life, and death of men and all living things, the commencement, middle, and end of all earthly matters, and the past, present, and future of universal space. In the same way, the universe was divided into three zones, the earth, air, and rest.

In the Bible history we find the following: The patriarchs held a threefold office; ADAM, NOAH, and SAUL, each had three sons ABRAHAM, ISAAC, and JACOB were particularly blessed of GOD; JOB had three friends; EZEKIEL named three just men; three holy men were cast into the fiery furnace; and JONAH was three days and three nights in the whale's belly. At the transfiguration three persons appeared with the Messiah; and he remained three days in the tomb. There were three orders of the priesthood, and three keepers of the door; the golden candlestick had three branches on each side, and there were three stones in each row of the High-Priest's breast-plate; the oxen which supported the molten sea were arranged by threes; and the Jews were commanded to assemble to the temple three times in a year, at the three grand festivals. MOSES appointed by divine command three cities of refuge, forbade the people to use the fruit of their newly-planted trees till after they were three years old, and made three witnesses necessary to establish a fact by which the life or property of another was called in question. In the remarkable history of BALAAM the ass spake after being struck three times, and the prophet conferred on ISRAEL three separate blessings. SAMSON thrice deceived DELILAH; HANNAH offered a sacrifice of three bullocks; SAMUEL gave a sign to SAUL, consisting of a combination of triads; and DAVID bowed thrice before JONATHAN. DAVID had three mighty men of valor; and when he had numbered the people of Israel, he was offered three alternatives, viz: Three years' famine, three months' at the mercy of his foes, or three days' pestilence. The principal religious festivals of the Jews were three; the camp of Israel was threefold, and the tribes were marshaled in divisions of three tribes each. There were three hallowed articles in the sanctuary, the candlestick, the table of shew bread, and the altar of incense. ELIJAH raised the widow's son by stretching himself upon the child three times; Samaria sustained a siege of three years; some of the kings of Israel and Judah reigned three years, some three months, and others only three days. REHOBOAM served GOD three years before he apostatized. The Jews fasted three days and three nights before they overcame HAMAN; their sacred writings had three divisions, the law, the prophets and the psalms; and they had three readings of Scripture, the text, the Mishna, and the Cabala.

In the Masonic ritual we find the following among many others: There are three qualifications of a candidate; and his assent is required to three interrogatories. The signs are threefold—the moral duties and the theological virtues are threefold. There are three qualifications for the servitude of an Entered Apprentice; three cardinal virtues; and three things which make a Lodge regular. The reports are threefold; three grand offerings are commemorated in Freemasonry; three places where the materials for the temple were prepared, the quarry, the forest, and the plain; three decorations to the pillars at the porch, emblematical of peace, unity, and plenty; three ways of preparing a brother; and three obligations in Ancient Masonry. There were three primitive Lodges; three ways to advance; three temples, the first built by SOLOMON and the two HIRAMS; the second by JOSHUA, ZERUBBABEL, and HAGGAI; and the third by HEROD, HILLEL, and SHAMMAI; three sojourners; three working-tools of a Royal Arch Mason; the temple had three apartments; and the length was thrice its breadth. There were three curtains in the temple, each of three colors; and there were three courts. There are three lessons taught, secrecy, morality, and good fellowship.

THE BREASTPLATE,

Worn by the High-Priest, is in imitation of that
worn by the High-Priest of Israel. The twelve
stones inserted therein allude to the twelve
tribes of Israel. The breastplate was called
the "Oracle of Urim and Thummim," which
signifies light and perfection, or revelation and
truth. By this oracle GOD was consulted by
the High-Priest of Israel upon all important
occasions. On the shoulders of the ephod worn
by the High-Priest were two onyx stones, which
served as buttons, by which the breastplate was
fastened. On these stones were engraven the
names of the twelve sons of JACOB, six on each—
the names of the elder on the right, those of
the younger on the left. These stones shone

with exceeding great brilliancy whenever the
sacrifices of the children of Israel were accepted
of GOD; so that all the people were satisfied of
his presence, assistance, and protection. When
the children of Israel forsook the landmarks of
their fathers, and followed after strange gods,
these stones ceased to shed forth their brilliancy,
in consequence of GOD'S displeasure at their
transgression of his law. In like manner, if
we, as Royal Arch Masons, expect to secure the
presence, assistance, and protection of the Great
I AM, we must apply our hearts unto wisdom,
and forsake not the landmarks which our fathers
set up.

THE ROYAL ARCH BANNER,

Which should be displayed in every regular
Chapter of Royal Arch Masons, is composed
of the four standards used to distinguish the
four principal tribes of the children of Israel,
who bore their banners through the wilderness,
viz: JUDAH, EPHRAIM, REUBEN, and DAN; and
under each of these principal standards were
assembled three tribes. There were, consequently, four divisions, with three tribes in each,
numbering 150,000, making in all 600,000

Holiness to the Lord

fighting men, or men of war. They marched
in a hollow square in traveling through the
wilderness, in order to guard and protect on
every side the sacred Ark of the Covenant.
The escutcheon or shield on the banner is
divided into four compartments by a green
cross, over which a narrow one of yellow is
placed. On each compartment formed by the
limbs of the cross is delineated the peculiar
emblem of one of these tribes, to wit: in the
first quarter, a golden lion on a field of blue,
representing JUDAH; in the second, a black ox,

on a field of gold, representing EPHRAIM; in the third, a man on a field of gold, representing REUBEN; and in the fourth, a golden eagle on a field of blue, representing DAN. Each of these is a component part of the hieroglyphic of the Cherubim, which represents the children of Israel; and they teach us that, in the erection of our second temple of "Holiness to the LORD," as well as in the prosecution of every great and important undertaking, we should display, as did our ancient brethren in the erection of the first temple, the strength and boldness of the lion, the patience of the ox, the swiftness of the eagle, and the intelligence of an upright and perfect man. As a crest, the banner is surmounted by the Ark of the Covenant, guarded by two Cherubim, with their wings touching in the center.

THE ARK OF THE COVENANT

Was a small chest or coffer, made by MOSES, AHOLIAB, and BEZALEEL, and was three feet nine inches long, two feet three inches wide and deep. It was constructed of shittim wood, covered with fine gold, and over all were the Cherubim with expanded wings. In the ark

were placed the pot of manna, AARON's rod, and the tables of stone, containing the decalogue, written by the finger of GOD. It was at first placed in the sanctuary of the tabernacle, and afterward deposited by King SOLOMON in the *Sanctum Sanctorum* of the temple, at the completion and dedication of that edifice, as you have seen represented in the Most Excellent Master's degree.

When the temple was destroyed by the Chaldeans, this ark was also destroyed, but Masonic tradition informs us that, before the completion of the temple, King SOLOMON—foreseeing that the children of Israel would, in process of time, deviate from the laws of GOD and provoke his displeasure, and that in consequence thereof, their city would be taken by their enemies and the temple be destroyed, and that so would forever perish the sacred treasures contained in the S∴ S∴

*　　*　　*　　*　　*　　*

The ark was placed on the MASONIC STONE OF FOUNDATION, which Masonic tradition says, was a perfect cube of white oriental porphyry, and on which was inscribed, in precious stones, the characters composing 　*　　*　　*　　*

This MASONIC STONE OF FOUNDATION our Grand Masters deposited in the S∴ V∴ underneath the S∴ S∴, as a pedestal, upon which to place the imitation of the Ark of the Covenant, and there it remained buried, until, at the rebuilding of the temple by ZERUBBABEL, it was discovered by three zealous sojourners, and subsequently made the corner-stone of the second temple. It was perfectly cubical in its form—all its sides being equal—symbolizing divine truth, which must alone direct and sustain us in our search after GOD and the true light.

Thus, within the imitation of the sacred Ark

of the Covenant, were deposited and safely kept the *sacred* treasures, for the space of 470 years, which should constantly remind us that our own breasts should afford an equally safe repository for the mysteries of the Order, that they may be handed down pure and unimpaired to the latest posterity.

The Cherubim guarding the Ark of the Covenant are to remind us that the sublime principles of our royal art have always had the immediate approval of heaven, and encourages us to redouble our assiduity in the practice of all those virtues which we are taught within the inner vail of the sanctuary.

The motto of Royal Arch Masonry, emblazoned on its banner, is the same which you observe on the forefront of the High-Priest's miter: "*Holiness to the Lord.*"

Up to this time you have been addressed and have addressed each other by the title of brother or brothers. You will now be called companions. And, companions, I trust that it has not been an idle or vain curiosity, that merely grasps at novelty, which has induced you to be exalted to this most sublime degree of Masonry, infinitely more important than all which have preceded it. It is calculated to impress upon our minds a firm belief in the existence and attributes of a supreme being, and it teaches us a due reverence for his great and holy name. It also brings to light many valuable *treasures* belonging to the Craft, after they had lain buried in darkness for the space of 470 years, and without a knowledge of which the Masonic character is incomplete.

The great, mysterious, and sacred name of Deity was communicated to MOSES at the B∴ B∴

*　　*　　*　　*　　*　　*

Thus promulgated to their law-giver by the Almighty, as his special appellation, this name of GOD became invested among the children of Israel with the profoundest veneration and awe; so much so, that they never presumed to pronounce it, except in a particular manner, and then only with solemn ceremonies and with the greatest reverence. Hence, in a long course of time, its true pronunciation became lost, except by the High-Priest, who once a year, on the day of atonement, pronounced the word three times in the sanctuary of the tabernacle.

*   *   *   *   *   *

After a series of important events, of which
you will find a particular account in the history
of the Kings of Judah and Israel, for the space
of 416 years from the consecration of the first
temple to its destruction by NEBUCHADNEZZAR,
we find that in the eleventh year of the reign of
ZEDEKIAH, King of Judah, NEBUZARADAN, Captain
of the Guard of the King of Babylon, went up,
besieged and took the city of Jerusalem, seized
all the holy vessels, the two famous brazen
pillars, and all the treasures of the king's house,
his palaces, and his princes.   He then set both
the temple and city on fire, overthrowing its
walls, towers, and fortresses, and totally level-
ing and razing it, until it became one thorough
desolation; and the remnant of the people that
escaped the sword carried he away captive to
the King of Babylon, where they remained
servants to him and his successors until the
reign of CYRUS, King of Persia, who, in the
first year of his reign, issued his famous proclamation, liberating the Hebrew captives, with
permission to return to their native country,
and rebuild the city and the house of the LORD.

Accordingly the principal people of the tribes of JUDAH and BENJAMIN, together with the priests and Levites, immediately departed for Jerusalem. They traveled over rough and rugged roads—over river and mountain—until, at length, after a toilsome and dreary march of more than four months, they arrived at that city, where they erected a tabernacle near the ruins of the old temple. This tabernacle, like that built by MOSES, was an oblong, situated due East and West, inclosed, and divided into apartments by four cross vails, the colors of which were blue, purple, scarlet, and white; and alluded to the four principal tribes of the children of Israel, who bore their banners through the wilderness. Guards were stationed at those vails, to see that none passed but such as were duly qualified—none being admitted into the presence of the Grand Council but the true descendants of the twelve tribes of Israel, who made themselves known by the same signs given by the LORD to MOSES when he commanded him to conduct the children of Israel out of the land of Egypt, and from the house of bondage.

In the tabernacle they set up the altar, and burned incense thereon day and night.

In the sanctuary the Grand Council, consisting of JOSHUA, the High-Priest, ZERUBBABEL, the king, and HAGGAI, the scribe, held their sessions and formed their plans.

Among those who returned were three of our ancient brethren, who were left behind in Babylon by the main body under ZERUBBABEL, and who afterward went to Jerusalem, to help, aid, and assist in the great and glorious work of rebuilding the house of the LORD, without the hope of fee or reward. Those three sojourners discovered and brought to light, as you have seen represented,

*   *   *   *   *   *

and, as a reward for their valuable labors, they were exalted to be Grand Masters of the Vails. Those three worthies you have had the honor to represent.

And now, companions, you have received all the instruction that pertains to our noble Craft.

You have ascended by regular gradations, to the summit of our sublime and royal art.

You have been conducted around the outer

courts of the temple, viewed its beautiful proportions, its massive pillars, its starry-decked canopy, its Mosaic pavement, its lights, jewels, and furniture.

You have been introduced into the middle chamber, and learned, by the example of our ancient brethren, to reverence the Sabbath day, and to keep it holy.

You have entered the unfinished S∴ S∴, and there, in the integrity and inflexible fidelity of the illustrious Tyrian, witnessed an example of firmness and fortitude never surpassed in the history of man.

You have wrought in the quarries, and exhibited suitable specimens of your skill, and have been taught how to receive, in a proper manner, your Masonic wages.

You have regularly passed the chair, and learned its important duties—a knowledge of which can alone qualify you to preside over the sons of light.

You have been present, and assisted at the completion and dedication of our mystic temple; and, for your zeal and fidelity to the Craft, have received the congratulatory title of Most Excellent Master.

You have now witnessed the mournful desolation of Zion, the sack and destruction of the city and temple of our GOD, and the utter loss, as the world supposed, of all those articles contained in the Holy of Holies.

You have seen the chosen people of GOD forced by a foreign despot from the pleasant groves and peaceful vineyards of their native Israel, and dragged into captivity on the banks of the far-off Euphrates.

But you have seen those afflicted sons of Zion visited, in the darkest night of their adversity, by a peaceful light from heaven, which guided them over rough and rugged roads to the scene of their former glory.

You have seen them enabled, by the signet of eternal truth, to pass the vails that interposed between them and their fondest hopes.

You have seen them successfully engaged in the great and glorious work of rebuilding the house of the LORD.

And, finally, you have seen the sacred treasures of the first temple brought to light, and the blessed book restored to the longing eyes of the devout Israelites, to be the rule and guide—the comfort and support—of the people of GOD throughout all future time.

And, my companions, if, in all these things, you have seen only a series of unmeaning rites —if the spirit of truth has not applied to your hearts the morals of these ceremonies—then, indeed, have we labored in vain, and you have spent your strength for nought.

But I am persuaded to believe better things of you. I trust that you have entered into the spirit of these solemn ceremonies, and understand the full import of these interesting symbols; that all the forms and ceremonies through which you have passed, from the moment you first trod the outer courts of the temple until your final reception within the vails, have impressed deeply on your minds the great and fundamental principles of our time-honored institution: for *then*, and *only then*, can you justly claim the noble name of Mason; *then*, and *only then*, can you feel that friendship, that union, that zeal, and that purity of heart, which should actuate every one who would appropriate to himself the proud title of a workman that needeth not to be ashamed.

CHARGE TO THE CANDIDATES

WORTHY COMPANIONS: By the consent and assistance of the members of this Chapter, you are now exalted to the sublime and honorable degree of Royal Arch Mason. The rites and mysteries developed in this degree have been handed down, through a chosen few, unchanged by time, and uncontrolled by prejudice; and we expect and trust they will be regarded by you with the same veneration, and transmitted with the same scrupulous purity to your successors.

No one can reflect on the ceremonies of gaining admission into this place without being forcibly struck with the important lessons which they teach. Here we are necessarily led to contemplate, with gratitude and admiration, the sacred source from whence all earthly comforts flow. Here we find additional inducements to continue steadfast and immovable in the discharge of our respective duties; and here we are bound by the most solemn ties to promote each other's welfare and correct each other's failings, by advice, admonition, and reproof. As it is our earnest desire, and a duty we

owe to our companions of this Order, that the
admission of every candidate into this Chapter
should be attended by the approbation of the
most scrutinizing eye, we hope always to
possess the satisfaction of finding none among
us but such as will promote, to the utmost of
their power, the great end of our institution.
By paying due attention to this determination,
we expect you will never recommend any candidate to this Chapter, whose abilities and
knowledge of the preceding degrees you cannot
freely vouch for, and whom you do not firmly
and confidently believe will fully conform to
the principles of our Order, and fulfill the
obligations of a Royal Arch Mason. While
such are our members, we may expect to be
united in one object, without lukewarmness,
inattention, or neglect; but zeal, fidelity, and af-
fection, will be the distinguishing characteristics
of our society; and that satisfaction, harmony,
and peace, may be enjoyed at our meetings
which no other society can afford.

CLOSING

♩

*   *   *   *   *

♫ ♩

THE Chapter is closed with solemn ceremonies by the Most Excellent High-Priest, who rehearses the following

PRAYER

By the *wisdom* of the Supreme High-Priest, may we be directed; by his *strength* may we be enabled, and by the *beauty* of virtue may we be incited to perform the obligations here enjoined on us; to keep inviolably the mysteries here unfolded to us; and invariably to practice all those duties out of the Chapter which are inculcated in it.—AMEN.

Response.—So mote it be.

*   *   *   *   *   *

ORDER OF HIGH-PRIESTHOOD

THE Order of High-Priesthood appertains to the office of High-Priest of a Royal Arch Chapter; and no one can be legally entitled to receive it, until he has been duly elected to preside as High-Priest in a regular Chapter of Royal Arch Masons. The Order should not be conferred when a less number than three duly-qualified High-Priests are present. Whenever the ceremony is performed in due and ample form, the assistance of at least nine High-Priests, who have received it, is requisite.

Though the High-Priest of every regular Royal Arch Chapter, having himself been duly qualified, can confer the Order under the preceding limitation as to number, yet it is desirable when circumstances will permit (in States where no Grand Convention has been organized), that it should be conferred by the Grand High-Priest of the Grand Royal Arch Chapter, or such Present or Past High-Priest as he may designate for that purpose. In such States, however, it will generally be found that a convention, notified to meet at the time of any convocation of the Grand Chapter, will afford the best opportunity of conferring this important and exalted degree of Masonry with appropriate solemnity.

A candidate desirous of receiving the Order of High-Priesthood makes a written request to his predecessor in office, or, when it can be done, to the Grand High-Priest, respectfully requesting that a convention of High-Priests may be called, for the purpose of conferring on him the Order. When the convention meets, and is duly organized, a certificate of the due election of the candidate to the office of High-Priest must be produced. This certificate is signed by his predecessor in office, attested by the Secretary and seal of the Chapter. On examination of this certificate, the qualifications of the candidate are ascertained. The solemn ceremonies of conferring the Order upon him then ensue. When ended, the presiding officer directs the Secretary of the convention to make a record of the proceedings, and return it to the Secretary of the Grand Chapter, to be by him laid before the Grand High-Priest, for the information of all whom it may concern. The convention of High-Priests is then closed in due form.

These regulations should never be dispensed with in the case of occasional or temporary organizations.

In most of the States permanent Grand Conventions have been formed with regular officers and stated meetings. In this way only can the Order obtain the rank and dignity to which its intrinsic merit entitles it, and it is to be hoped that measures will be speedily taken to place the Order in all the States on a solid and permanent basis.

If the Order is conferred by three High-Priests, under a temporary organization, the meeting is said to be a "Convention." If a State body is established, its proper title is "The Grand Convention."

It is the duty of every companion, as soon after his election to the office of High-Priest as is consistent with his personal convenience, to apply for admission to the Order of High-Priesthood, that he may be fully qualified properly to govern his Chapter.

The robes, collars, and jewels are the same as those of the Royal Arch degree.

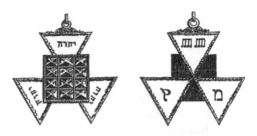

The jewel of a Past High-Priest consists of a plate of gold, in the form of a triple triangle, a breastplate being placed over the points of union. In front, the face of each triangle is inscribed with the tetragrammaton, יהוה; on the other side, the upper triangle has the following mystical notation: ♪♪♪♪ ♪♪♪♪♪ the two lower triangles have the Hebrew letters מ and ק inserted upon them. Each side of each triangle should be one inch in length, and may be ornamented at the fancy of the wearer. The breastplate may be plainly engraved or set with stones.

Candidates receiving this Order are said to be "anointed into the Holy Order of the High-Priesthood."

A convention of High-Priests is "dedicated to MEL-CHIZEDEK."

OFFICERS

THE Officers of a Grand Convention of anointed High-Priests should be as follows:

 1. M. E. PRESIDENT;

 2. E. VICE-PRESIDENT;

 3. E. CHAPLAIN;

 4. E. TREASURER;

 5. E. RECORDER;

 6. E. MASTER OF CEREMONIES;

 7. E. CONDUCTOR;

 8. E. HERALD;

 9. E. STEWARD;

To which it will be found convenient, in practice, to add a SENTINEL.

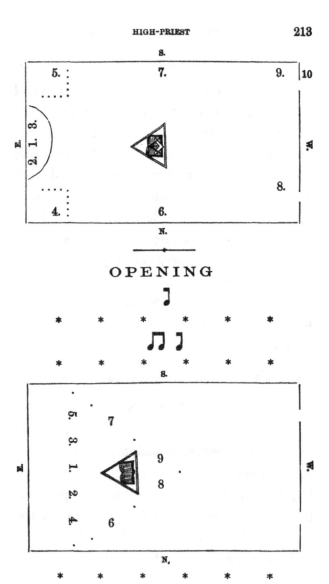

DEVOTIONS

OH, thou Supreme High-Priest of heaven and earth, enlighten us, we beseech thee, with the knowledge of thy truth, and grant that the members of this convention, and all others who are teachers in Israel, may be endowed with wisdom to understand and to explain the mysteries of our Order. Be with us in all our assemblies, guide us in the paths of rectitude, and enable us to keep all thy statutes and commandments, while life shall last, and finally bring us to the true knowledge of thy holy and mighty name —AMEN.

Response.—So mote it be.

Or the following may be appropriately rehearsed:

LESSON

THE spirit of the LORD JEHOVAH is upon me; because the LORD hath anointed me to preach good tidings unto the meek; he hath sent me to bind up the broken-hearted, to proclaim liberty to the captives, and the opening of the prison to them that are bound;

To proclaim the acceptable year of the LORD,

and the day of vengeance of our GOD; to comfort all that mourn;

To appoint unto them that mourn in Zion, to give unto them beauty for ashes, the oil of joy for mourning, the garment of praise for the spirit of heaviness; that they might be called Trees of Righteousness. The planting of the LORD, that he might be glorified.—ISAIAH, lxi., 1-3.

*   *   *   *   *   *

RECEPTION

THE candidate must present a certificate of his election to the office of High-Priest of a Chapter of Royal Arch Masons, which should be in the following form:

TO ALL WHOM IT MAY CONCERN.

This is to certify that Companion .... was, on the .... day of ......, A. D. 1 ., A. I. 2 ..,* duly and constitutionally elected to the office of High-Priest of .... Chapter, No. .., working under charter from the M. E. Grand Royal Arch Chapter of the State of ....

Given under my hand, and the seal of the Chapter, this .... day of ......, A. D. 1 .., A. L. 2 ...

[SEAL.] ——— ———, *Secretary.*

* The Royal Arch Date (A. I., Year of Discovery,) is found by adding 530 to the Year of our Lord.

This certificate must be regularly authenticated by the signature of the Secretary, and the seal of the Chapter.

But should the candidate, for sufficient reason assigned, be unable to produce such a certificate, then a certificate from the Grand Secretary of the Grand Royal Arch Chapter under which the candidate has served as High-Priest, certifying to the facts from the record, will be considered lawful information, and may be used accordingly.

If the candidate is found worthy, the ceremonies follow in ample form.

FIRST CLAUSE

*   *   *   *   *   *

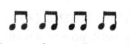

*   *   *   *   *   *

The following passage of Scripture is read by the Excellent Chaplain during the ceremony:

And it came to pass in the days of AMRAPHEL, King of Shinar; ARIOCH, King of Ellasar; CHEDORLAOMER, King of ELAM, and TIDAL, King of Nations; that these made war with BERA, King of Sodom; and with BIRSHA, King of Gomorrah, SHINAB, King of Admah; and SHEMEBER, King of Zeboiim, and the King of Bela, which is ZOAR.

*   *   1   *   *

All these were joined together in the vale of Siddim, which is the Salt Sea.

Twelve years they served CHEDORLAOMER, and in the thirteenth year they rebelled.

And in the fourteenth year came CHEDOR-LAOMER, and the kings that were with him, and smote the Rephaims in Ashteroth, and the Zuzims in Ham, and the Emims in Shaveh Kiriathaim, and the Horites in their Mount Seir, unto El-paran, which is by the wilderness.

*   *   2   *   *

And they returned, and came to Enmishpat, which is Kadesh, and smote all the country of the Amalekites, and also the Amorites, that dwelt in Hazezon-tamar.

And there went out the King of Sodom, and the King of Gomorrah, and the King of Admah, and the King of Zeboiim, and the King of Bela, and they joined battle with them in the vale of Siddim; with CHEDORLAOMER, the King of Elam; and with TIDAL, King of Nations; and AMRAPHEL, King of Shinar; and ARIOCH, King of Ellasar; four kings with five.

*   *   3   *   *

And the vale of Siddim was full of slime pits; and the Kings of Sodom and Gomorrah fled and fell there; and they that remained fled to the mountain.

And they took all the goods of Sodom and Gomorrah, and all their victuals, and went their way.

And they took Lot, Abram's brother's son, who dwelt in Sodom, and his goods, and departed.

*   *   4   *   *

And there came one that had escaped, and told Abram the Hebrew; for he dwelt in the plain of *Mamre* the Amorite, brother of Eshcol, and brother of Aner; and these were confederate with Abram. And when Abram heard that his brother was taken captive, he armed his trained servants, born in his own house, three hundred and eighteen, and pursued them unto Dan. And he divided himself against them, he and his servants, by night, and smote them, and pursued them unto Hobah, which is on the left hand of Damascus.

* * 5 * *

And he brought back all the goods, and also brought again his brother LOT, and his goods, and the women also, and the people. And the King of Sodom went out to meet him (after his return from the slaughter of *Chedorlaomer*, and of the kings that were with him), at the valley of Shaveh, which is the king's dale. And *Melchizedek*, King of Salem, brought forth bread and wine; and he was the *Priest of the Most High God*.

* * 6 * *

And he blessed him, and said, Blessed be ABRAM of the Most High GOD, possessor of heaven and earth ; and blessed be the Most High GOD, which hath delivered thine enemies into thy hand. And he gave him tithes of all. And the King of Sodom said unto ABRAM, Give me the persons, and take the goods to thyself.

* * 7 * *

And ABRAM said to the King of Sodom, I have lifted up mine hand unto the LORD, the Most High GOD, the possessor of heaven and earth, that I will not take *from a thread even to a shoe latchet*, and that I will not take anything that is thine, lest thou shouldest say, I have made Abram rich; save only that which the young men have eaten, and the portion of the men which went with me, Aner, Eshcol, and Mamre; let them take their portion—Gen. xiv.

*   *   8   *   *

This entire passage of Scripture should be read, accompanied by solemn ceremonies. The events which it describes should be carefully noted, as many things in the ritual are made to depend upon its recital, and if abbreviated, the candidate will fail to comprehend the full symbolism intended to be displayed in the ceremonies.

From a Thread to a Shoe Latchet

Sandals were worn by all classes of society in Palestine, even by the very poor, and both the sandal and the thong, or shoe latchet, were so cheap and common that they passed into a proverb for the most insignificant thing, in which sense it is used in Gen. xiv., 2, 3.

The thread was a fillet used by women to tie up their hair, and was also used proverbially to designate the cheapest or a valueless thing. The force of this expression will be readily understood as employed in the ritual.

*   *   *   *   *   *

SECOND CLAUSE

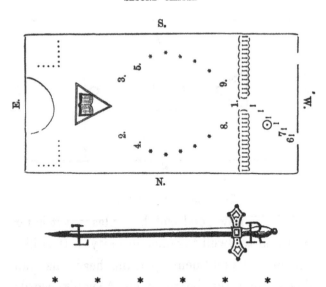

Blessed be ABRAM of the Most High GOD, possessor of heaven and earth. And blessed

be the Most High GOD, which hath delivered
thine enemies into thy hands.

*   *   *   *   *   *

Such was the blessing which the King of Salem, Priest of the
Most High GOD, invoked on Abram the father of the faithful; and
such will be the blessing vouchsafed to every faithful High-Priest
of a Chapter, who strives to walk in the fear of the Almighty, and
who sets before his companions, in his own life, an example of
uprightness and integrity. Such an one will, indeed. be blessed
of the Most High GOD.

*   *   *   *   *   *

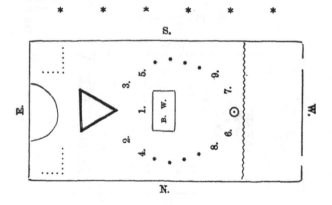

The Communion of Brethren

Behold, how good and how pleasant it is for
brethren to dwell together in unity! It is like
the precious ointment upon the head, that ran
down upon the beard, even AARON'S beard;
that went down to the skirts of his garment;
as the dew of Hermon, and as the dew that

descended upon the mountains of Zion; for there the LORD commanded a blessing, even life for evermore.—PSALM cxxxiii.

*   *   *   *   *   *

Behold, bless ye the LORD, all ye servants of the LORD, which by night stand in the house of the LORD. Lift up your hands in the Sanctuary, and bless the LORD. The LORD that made heaven and earth bless thee out of Zion.— PSALM cxxxiv.

*   *   *   *   *   *

Among most of the ancient heathen nations it was a custom strictly observed, that those who sacrificed to the gods should eat of the sacrifice. It is an interesting question from whence this custom was derived. Many scholars are of the opinion that this universal custom of sacrificing to the gods was derived originally from the establishment of a sacrificial system by the divine command at some period anterior to the foundation of the Levitical System. It will be observed that the Mosaic account speaks of sacrifices as something already existing, and apparently seeks to govern rather than invent them.

Under the Jewish law, it was commanded that those who sacrificed should eat before the LORD. It betokened the enjoyment of communion with GOD. So in thus partaking together of the Paschal Supper, those who ate together were at once to commune with GOD, and evince a mutual love and confidence toward each other. Hence a refusal to eat with one implied an entire and absolute separation. The Hebrews would not eat with the Egyptians* nor with the Samaritans.†. To eat a meal together is now regarded in the East as a pledge of mutual confidence and friend-

* Genesis, xliii., 32.   † John, iv., 9.

ship. The communion of brethren is therefore a public attestation
to the sincerity of purpose with which those who unite in it have
thus far proceeded in the solemn services of the Order, and a
solemn pledge of that mutual love, assistance, and protection
which is enjoined upon all who take upon themselves its covenant.

*   *   *   *   *

The anointment of a High-Priest is preceded by the
following

PRAYER

MOST Holy and glorious LORD GOD, the great
High-Priest of heaven and earth! we approach
thee with reverence, and implore thy blessing
on thy servant, our companion, now prostrate
before thee; fill his heart with thy fear, that
his tongue and actions may pronounce thy
glory. Make him steadfast in thy service;
grant him firmness of mind; animate his heart,
and strengthen his endeavors; may he teach
thy judgments, and thy laws; and may the
incense he shall put before thee, upon thine
altar, prove an acceptable sacrifice unto thee.
Make him a true and faithful teacher of the
companions over whom he has been chosen to
preside, and enable him to perform the duties
of his exalted office with fidelity and zeal.
Bless him, O LORD, and bless the work of his

hands. Accept us in mercy. Hear thou from heaven, thy dwelling place, and forgive our transgressions.

Response—So mote it be.—AMEN.

*   *   *   *   *   *

The President will recite the following

BENEDICTION

THE LORD bless thee and keep thee; the LORD make his face to shine upon thee, and be gracious unto thee; the LORD lift up his countenance upon thee, and give thee peace.

Response—So mote it be.—AMEN.

*   *   *   *   *   *

Anointing the body or head with oil was a common practice with the Jews and other Oriental nations. It was a rite of inauguration into each of the three typical offices of the Jewish commonwealth. Prophets were occasionally anointed to their office. Priests, at the first institution of the Levitical Priesthood, were all anointed to their offices, the sons of AARON as well as AARON himself; but afterward anointing seems not to have been repeated at the consecration of ordinary priests, but to have been especially reserved for the High-Priest. Anointing in like manner was the principal and divinely-appointed ceremony in the inauguration of the Jewish kings; indeed, so preëminently did it belong to the kingly office, that the "LORD's anointed" was a common designation of the theocratic king. DAVID was thrice anointed to be king; privately by SAMUEL, again over Judah at Hebron, and lastly over the whole nation. It was customary at festivals and on other great occasions to anoint the head with fragrant oils, and hence it came to be a mark of respect and a sign of joy. It was in all cases of official anointing viewed as a symbol of sanctification and of dedication to the service of GOD, or to the holy and sacred use. So reference is made to it here, as a symbolical consecrating or setting apart of the neophyte to the honorable and responsible position of High-Priesthood in Royal Arch Masonry.

*　　*　　*　　*　　*　　*

The following charge is delivered to the candidate by the President:

*　　*　　*　　*　　*　　*

*　　*　　* Remember that the responsibilities of this Holy Order rest not alone upon the officers, but equally upon the individual members of the Order; a dereliction from duty being equally destructive in the one case as the other. As you value, then, your honor as a man and Mason; as you prize the purity and permanency of the Order; as you fear to displease GOD ALMIGHTY, whose name you have so solemnly invoked, keep inviolate every pledge you have made, and perform with fidelity every duty to which you have become bound.

Be as swift as the eagle to do every good work to a companion anointed High-Priest; be as patient as the ox with the foibles and errors of your companions; let the Lion of the tribe of Judah be the symbol of your strength and boldness in the cause of truth and justice; but, above all, continuallv strive to set before your companions of the Royal Craft the bright example of an upright and perfect man. Let *Holiness to the Lord* be engraven upon all your thoughts, words, and actions; and may GOD, who dwelleth between the cherubim, finally, after this painful life is ended, admit you into the Sanctuary, eternal in the Heaven.

* * * * * *

CLOSING

* * * *

DEVOTIONS

SAVE us, O LORD our GOD, and gather us from amongst the nations, to give thanks unto thy holy name, to triumph in thy praise. Blessed be the Lord God of Israel from eternity to eternity; and let all the people say, Amen. Praise ye the Lord.—Psalm cvi., 47, 48.

Or the following passages of Scripture may be read instead:

For this Melchizedek, King of Salem, Priest of the Most High God, who met Abraham returning from the slaughter of the kings, and blessed him; to whom also Abraham gave a tenth part of all, first being by interpretation King of righteousness, and after that also King of Salem, which is King of peace; without father, without mother, without descent, having neither beginning of days, nor end of life; but made like unto the Son of God; abideth a priest continually. Now consider how great this man was, unto whom even the patriarch Abraham gave the tenth of the spoils. And verily, they that are of the sons of Levi, who receive the office of the priesthood, have a commandment to take tithes of the people according to the law, that is, of their brethren, though they come out of the loins of Abraham. For he testifieth, Thou art a priest forever after the order of

MELCHIZEDEK. And inasmuch as not without an oath he was made priest: For those priests (under the Levitical law) were made without an oath; but this with an oath, by him that said unto him, the LORD sware, and will not repent, Thou art a priest forever, after the order of MELCHIZEDEK.—HEBREWS, vii.

* * * * *

* * * * *

CEREMONIES OF THE ORDER

---

1. The new Chapter will meet in its hall, and open on the Royal Arch degree.

2. The Grand Chapter will meet in an adjoining room, and organize.

3. A committee from the new Chapter will inform the Grand Officers that their Chapter is prepared to receive them.

4. The Grand Officers will move in procession, conducted by the committee, to the hall of the Chapter, in the following order:

Grand Sentinel;

Representatives of Subordinate Chapters, according to seniority, by threes, triangular;

Masters of the Three Vails;

Orator, Chaplain, and other Clergy;

Grand Secretary, Grand Treasurer, and Grand Royal Arch Captain;

Grand P. Sojourner, Grand Captain of the Host, and Deputy Grand High-Priest;

One Companion carrying the Pot of Incense;

Four Companions carrying the Ark;

Three Companions carrying Lights, triangularly;

Grand Scribe, Grand King, and Grand High-Priest.

5. When the Grand High-Priest enters, the grand honors are given, and the officers of the new Chapter resign their seats to the Grand Officers, and take their stations on the left.

6. An Ode may be sung.

7. All kneeling, the Grand Chaplain will deliver the following

PRAYER

ALMIGHTY and Supreme High-Priest of heaven and earth, who is there in heaven but thee, and who upon earth can stand in competition with thee? Thy *Omniscient* mind brings all things in review—past, present, and to come; thine *Omnipotent* arm directs the movements of the vast creation; thine *Omnipresent* eye pervades the secret recesses of every heart; thy boundless beneficence supplies us with every comfort and enjoyment; and thine unspeakable perfections and glory surpass the understanding of the children of men! Our Father, who art in heaven, we invoke thy benediction upon the purposes of our present assembly. Let this Chapter be established to thine honor; let its officers be endowed with wisdom to discern, and fidelity to pursue, its true interests; let its members be ever-mindful of the duty they owe to their God; the obedience they owe to their superiors; the love they owe to their equals, and the good-will they owe to all mankind. Let this Chapter be consecrated to thy glory, and its members ever exemplify their love to God by their beneficence to man.

Glory be to God on high.

Response—So mote it be.—AMEN.

8. Address by the Grand High-Priest.

9. The Grand Captain of the Host will then form the officers of the new Chapter in front of the Grand High-Priest.

10. The Deputy Grand High-Priest then rises, and informs the Grand High-Priest that

A number of Companions, duly instructed in the sublime mysteries, being desirous of promoting the honor, and propagating the principles of the Art, have applied to the Grand Chapter for a warrant to constitute a new Chapter of Royal Arch Masons, which, having been obtained, they are now assembled for the purpose of being constituted, and having their officers installed in due and ancient form.

11. The Grand High-Priest directs the Grand Secretary to read the warrant; which being done,

12. The Grand High-Priest rises, and says:

By virtue of the high powers in me vested, I do form you, my respected Companions, into a regular Chapter of Royal Arch Masons. From henceforth you are authorized and empowered to open and hold a Lodge of Mark Masters, Past Masters, and Most Excellent Masters, and a Chapter of Royal Arch Masons; and to do and perform all such things as thereunto may appertain; conforming, in all your doings, to *the General Grand Royal Arch Constitution and** the general regulations of the State Grand Chapter. And may the GOD of your fathers be with, guide, and direct you in all your doings.

GRAND HONORS

13. The furniture, clothing, jewels, implements, utensils, etc., belonging to the Chapter (having been previously placed in the center, in front of the Grand High-Priest,) are now uncovered, and the dedication proceeds:

DEDICATION

THE Grand Chaplain, with the pot of incense in his hands, says:

To our Most Excellent Patron, ZERUBBABEL, we solemnly dedicate this Chapter. May the

---

* Those words marked in italics, and the same words similarly designated in other parts of these services, may be omitted in those States which are not under the jurisdiction of the General Grand Chapter.

blessing of our Heavenly High-Priest descend and rest upon its members, and may their felicity be immortal. Glory be to GOD on high.

As it was in the beginning, is now, and ever shall be, without end!—AMEN.

Response—So mote it be.

INSTALLATION

THE Deputy Grand High-Priest will then present the first officer of the (new) Chapter to the Grand High-Priest, saying:

Most Excellent Grand High-Priest: I present you my worthy Companion, —— —— (nominated in the warrant), to be installed High-Priest of this (new) Chapter. I find him to be skillful in the royal art, and attentive to the moral precepts of our forefathers, and have therefore no doubt but he will discharge the duties of his office with fidelity.

The Grand High-Priest then addresses him as follows:

Most Excellent Companion: I feel much satisfaction in performing my duty on the present

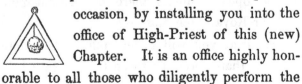 occasion, by installing you into the office of High-Priest of this (new) Chapter. It is an office highly honorable to all those who diligently perform the

important duties annexed to it. Your reputed Masonic knowledge, however, precludes the necessity of a particular enumeration of those duties. I shall, therefore, only observe, that by a frequent recurrence to the Constitution, and general regulations and constant practice of the several sublime lectures and charges, you will be best able to fulfill them; and I am confident that the Companions who are chosen to preside with you will give strength to your endeavors, and support your exertions. I shall now propose certain questions to you, relative to the duties of your office, and to which I must request your unequivocal answer.

I. Do you solemnly promise that you will redouble your endeavors to correct the vices, purify the morals, and promote the happiness of those of your Companions who have attained this sublime degree?

II. That you will never suffer your Chapter to be opened unless there be present nine regular Royal Arch Masons?

III. That you will never suffer either more or less than three brethren to be exalted in your Chapter at one and the same time?

IV. That you will not exalt any one to this degree who has not shown a charitable and humane disposition; or who has not made a considerable proficiency in the foregoing degrees?

V. That you will promote the general good of our Order, and, on all proper occasions, be ready to give and receive instructions, and particularly from the General and State Grand Officers?

VI. That, to the utmost of your power, you will preserve the solemnities of our ceremonies, and behave, in open Chapter, with the most profound respect and reverence, as an example to your Companions?

VII. That you will not acknowledge or have intercourse with any Chapter that does not work under a constitutional warrant or dispensation?

VIII. That you will not admit any visitor into your Chapter who has not been exalted in a Chapter legally constituted, without his being first formally healed?

IX. That you will observe and support such by-laws as may be made by your Chapter, in conformity to *General Grand Royal Arch Constitution, and* the general regulations of the Grand Chapter?

X. That you will pay due respect and obedience to the instructions of the *General and* State Grand Officers, particularly relating to the several lectures and charges, and will resign the chair to them, severally, when they may visit your Chapter?

XI. That you will support and observe the *General Grand Royal Arch Constitution and the* general regulations of the Grand Royal Arch Chapter, under whose authority you act?

XII. That you will bind your successor in office to the observance of the same rules to which you have now assented?

Do you submit to all these things, and do you promise to observe and practice them faithfully?

These questions being answered in the affirmative, the Companions all kneel, and the Grand Chaplain repeats the following

PRAYER

Most Holy and glorious LORD GOD, the Great High-Priest of heaven and earth! we approach thee with reverence, and implore thy blessing on (the) Companion appointed to preside over this new assembly, and now prostrate before thee; fill his heart with thy fear, that his tongue and actions may pronounce thy glory. Make him steadfast in thy service; grant him firmness of mind; animate his heart, and strengthen his endeavors; may he teach thy judgments and thy laws; and may the incense he shall put before thee, upon thine altar, prove an acceptable sacrifice unto thee. Bless him, O LORD, and bless the work of his hands. Accept us in mercy. Hear thou from heaven, thy dwelling place, and forgive our transgressions.

Response—So mote it be.

The Grand High-Priest will then cause the High-Priest elect to be invested with his clothing, badges, etc.; after which, he will address him as follows:

Most Excellent: In consequence of your cheerful acquiescence with the charges, which you have heard recited, you are qualified for installation as the High-Priest of this Royal Arch Chapter; and it is incumbent upon me, on this occasion, to point out some of the particulars appertaining to your office, duty, and dignity.

The High-Priest of every Chapter has it in special charge to see that the by-laws of his Chapter, *as well as the General Grand Royal Arch Constitution, and* all the regulations of the Grand Chapter, are duly observed; that all the officers of his Chapter perform the duties of their respective offices faithfully, and are examples of diligence and industry to their Companions; that true and accurate records of all the proceedings of the Chapter are kept by the Secretary; that the Treasurer keeps and renders exact and just accounts of all the moneys and other property belonging to the Chapter; that the regular returns be made annually to the Grand Chapter; and that the annual dues to the Grand Chapter be regularly and punctually paid. He has the right and authority of calling his Chapter together at pleasure, upon any emergency or occurrence which, in his judgment, may require their meeting. It is his privilege and duty, together with the King and Scribe, to attend the meetings of the Grand Chapter, either in person or by proxy; and the well-being of the institution requires that this duty should on no occasion be omitted.

The office of High-Priest is a station highly honorable to all those who diligently perform the important duties annexed to it. By a frequent recurrence to the Constitution and general regulations, and a constant practice of the several sublime lectures and charges, you will be best enabled to fulfill those duties; and I am confident that the Companions who are chosen to preside with you will give strength to your endeavors and support to your exertions.

Let the *Miter*, with which you are invested, remind you of the dignity of the office you sustain, and its inscription impress upon your mind a sense of your dependence upon GOD; that perfection is not given unto man upon earth, and that perfect holiness belongeth alone unto the LORD.

The *Breastplate* with which you are decorated, in imitation of that upon which were engraven the names of the twelve tribes, and worn by the High-Priest of Israel, is to teach you that

you are always to bear in mind your responsibility to the laws and ordinances of the
institution, and that the honor and interests of
your Chapter and its members should be always
near your heart.

The *various colors* of the *Robes* you wear are
emblematical of every grace and virtue which
can adorn and beautify the human mind; each
of which will be briefly illustrated in the course
of the charges to be delivered to your subordinate officer.

I now deliver into your hands the *Charter*
under which you are to work. You will receive
it as a sacred deposit, and never permit it to
be used for any other purposes than those
expressed in it.

I present you with the *Book of the Law*, the
Great Light in every degree of Masonry. The
doctrines contained in this sacred volume create
in us a belief in the dispensations of Divine
Providence, which belief strengthens our FAITH,
and enables us to ascend the first step of the
Grand Masonic Ladder. This faith naturally
produces in us a HOPE of becoming partakers

of the promises expressed in this inestimable gift of GOD to man; which hope enables us to ascend the second step. But the third and last, being CHARITY, comprehends the former, and will continue to exert its influence, when Faith shall be lost in sight, and Hope in complete enjoyment.

I present you with the *Constitution* (of the General Grand Royal Arch Chapter); the Rules and Regulations of the Grand Royal Arch Chapter of this State; and, also, with the *By-Laws* of your Chapter. You will cause all these to be frequently read and punctually obeyed.

And now, Most Excellent, permit me, in behalf of the Craft here assembled, to offer you our most sincere congratulations on your accession to the honorable station you now fill. I doubt not you will govern with such order and regularity as to convince your companions that their partiality has not been misplaced.

Companions of .... Chapter, ...: Behold your High-Priest. [*They rise and bow, or, if the Installation be not public, salute him with the honors of Royal Arch Masonry.*] Recollect that the prosperity of your Chapter will as much depend on your support, assistance and obedience, as on his assiduity, information and wisdom.

The Grand Captain of the Host will then present the second officer to the Deputy Grand High-Priest, who will present him to the Grand High-Priest. The Grand High-Priest will then ask him whether he has attended to the ancient charges and regulations before recited to his superior officer; if he answers in the affirmative, he is asked whether he fully and freely assents to the same; if he answers in the affirmative, the Grand High-Priest directs his Deputy to invest him with his clothing, etc., and then addresses him as follows:

CHARGE TO THE KING

Excellent Companion: The important station to which you are elected in this Chapter requires

from you exemplary conduct; its duties demand your most assiduous attention; you are to second and support your chief in all the requirements of his office ; and should casualties at any time prevent his attendance, you are to succeed him in the performance of his duties. Your badge (the *Level*, surmounted by a *Crown*,) should remind you that, although you are the representative of a King, and exalted by office above your companions, yet that you remain upon a level with them, as respects your duty to GOD, your neighbor, and yourself; that you are equally bound with them to be obedient to the laws and ordinances of the institution, to be charitable, humane and just, and to seek every occasion of doing good.

Your office teaches a striking lesson of humility. The institutions of political society teach us to consider the King as the chief of created beings, and that the first duty of his subjects is to obey his mandates; but the institutions of our sublime degrees, by placing the King in a situation subordinate to the High-Priest, teaches us that our duty to GOD is paramount to all other duties, and should ever claim the priority of our obedience to man; and that, however strongly we may be bound to obey the laws of civil society, yet that those laws, to be just, should never intermeddle with matters of conscience, nor dictate articles of faith.

The *Scarlet Robe*, an emblem of imperial

dignity, should remind you of the paternal concern you should ever feel for the welfare of your Chapter, and the *fervency* and *zeal* with which you should endeavor to promote its prosperity.

In presenting to you the *Crown*, which is an emblem of royalty, I would remind you that to reign sovereign in the hearts and affections of men must be far more grateful to a generous and benevolent mind than to rule over their lives and fortunes; and that, to enable you to enjoy this preeminence with honor and satisfaction, you must subject your own passions and prejudices to the dominion of reason and charity.

You are entitled to the second seat in the council of your Companions. Let the bright example of your illustrious predecessor in the Grand Council at Jerusalem stimulate you to the faithful discharge of your duties; and when the King of kings shall summon you into his immediate presence, from his hand may you receive a CROWN OF GLORY, which shall never fade away.

CHARGE TO THE SCRIBE

Excellent Companion: The office of Scribe, to which you are elected, is very important and respectable. In the absence of your superior officers, you are bound to succeed them, and 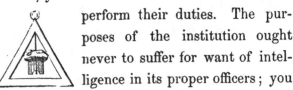 perform their duties. The purposes of the institution ought never to suffer for want of intelligence in its proper officers; you will therefore perceive the necessity there is of your possessing such qualifications as will enable you to accomplish those duties which are incumbent upon you, in your appropriate station, as well as those which may occasionally devolve on you by the absence of your superiors.

The *Purple Robe*, with which you are invested, is an emblem of UNION, and is calculated to remind you that the harmony and unanimity of the Chapter should be your constant aim; and to this end you are studiously to avoid all occasions of giving offense, or countenancing anything that may create divisions or dissensions. You are, by all means in your power, to endeavor to establish a permanent union and good understanding among all orders and degrees of Masonry; and as the glorious sun, at its meridian hight, dispels the mists and clouds which obscure the horizon, so may your exertions tend to dissipate the gloom of jealousy and discord whenever they may appear.

Your badge (a *Plumb-rule*, surmounted by a *Turban*,) is an emblem of rectitude and vigilance; and while you stand as a watchman upon the tower, to guard your companions against the approach of those enemies of human felicity, *intemperance* and *excess*, let this faithful monitor ever remind you to walk uprightly in your station; admonishing and animating your companions to fidelity and industry while at labor, and to temperance and moderation while at refreshment. And when the great Watchman of Israel, whose eye never slumbers nor sleeps, shall relieve you from your post on earth, may he permit you in heaven to participate in that food and refreshment which is

> "Such as the saints in glory love,
> And such as angels eat."

CHARGE TO THE CAPTAIN OF THE HOST

Companion: The office with which you are intrusted is of high importance, and demands

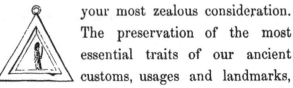

your most zealous consideration. The preservation of the most essential traits of our ancient customs, usages and landmarks, are within your province; and it is indispensably necessary that the part assigned to you, in the immediate practice of our rites and ceremonies, should be perfectly understood and correctly administered.

Your office corresponds with that of *Marshal*, or Master of Ceremonies. You are to superintend all processions of your Chapter, when moving as a distinct body, either in public or private; and as the world can only judge of our private discipline by our public deportment, you will be careful that the utmost order and decorum be observed on all such occasions. You will ever be attentive to the commands of your chief, and always near at hand to see them duly executed. I invest you with the badge of your office, and presume that you will give to your duties all that study and attention which their importance demands.

CHARGE TO THE PRINCIPAL SOJOURNER

Companion: The office confided to you, though subordinate in degree, is equal in importance to

any in the Chapter, that of your chief alone excepted. Your office corresponds with that *of Senior Deacon,* in the preparatory degrees.

Among the duties required of you the preparation and introduction of candidates are not the least. As, in our intercourse with the world, experience teaches that first impressions are often the most durable, and the most difficult to eradicate, so it is of great importance, in all cases, that those impressions should be correct and just; hence it is essential that the officer who brings the blind by a way that they knew not, and leads them in paths that they have not known, should always be well qualified to make darkness light before them, and crooked things straight.

Your robe of office is an emblem of humility; and teaches that, in the prosecution of a laudable undertaking, we should never decline taking any part that may be assigned us, although it may be the most difficult or dangerous.

The *rose-colored tesselated border*, adorning the robe. is an emblem of ardor and perseverance, and signifies that when we have engaged in a virtuous course, notwithstanding all the impediments, hardships and trials we may be destined to encounter, we should endure them all with fortitude, and ardently persevere unto the end ; resting assured of receiving, at the termination of our labors, a noble and glorious reward. Your past exertions will be considered as a pledge of your future assiduity in the faithful discharge of you duties.

CHARGE TO THE ROYAL ARCH CAPTAIN

Companion : The well-known duties of your station require but little elucidation. Your

office in the preparatory degrees corresponds with that of *Junior Deacon*. It is your province, conjointly with the Captain of the :nd the examination of all visitors, and to take care that none are permitted to enter the Chapter but such as have *traveled the rugged path* of trial, and evinced their title to our favor and friendship. You will be attentive to obey the commands of the Captain of the Host during the introduction of *strangers* among the workmen; and should they be permitted to pass your post, may they, by him, be introduced into the presence of the Grand Council.

The *White Banner*, intrusted to your care, is emblematical of that purity of heart and rectitude of conduct which ought to actuate all those who pass the white vail of the sanctuary. I give it to you strongly in charge, never to suffer any one to pass your post without the *Signet of Truth*. I present you the badge of your office, in expectation of your performing your duties with intelligence, assiduity and propriety.

CHARGE TO THE MASTER OF THE THIRD VAIL

Companion: I present you with the *Scarlet Banner*, which is the ensign of your office, and with a sword to protect and defend the same. The rich and beautiful color of your banner is emblematical of fervency and zeal;

it is the appropriate color of the Royal Arch
degree. It admonishes us that we should be
fervent in the exercise of our devotion to GOD,
and zealous in our endeavors to promote the
happiness of man.

CHARGE TO THE MASTER OF THE SECOND VAIL

Companion: I invest you with the *Purple
Banner*, which is the ensign of your office, and

arm you with a sword, to enable
you to maintain its honor. The
color of your banner is produced
by a due mixture of *blue* and *scarlet;* the former of which is the characteristic
color of the *symbolic*, or *first three degrees of
Masonry*, and the latter that of the *Royal Arch
degree*. It is an emblem of UNION. and is the
characteristic color of the intermediate degrees.
It admonishes us to cultivate and improve
that spirit of union and harmony between the
brethren of the symbolic degrees and the
Companions of the sublime degrees which
should ever distinguish the members of a
society founded upon the principles of everlasting truth and universal philanthropy.

CHARGE TO THE MASTER OF THE FIRST VAIL

Companion: I invest you with the *Blue Banner*, which is the ensign of your office, and a sword for its defense and protection. The color of your banner is one of the most durable and beautiful in nature. It is the appropriate color adopted and worn by our ancient brethren of the three symbolic degrees, and is the *peculiar characteristic* of an institution which has stood the test of ages, and which is as much distinguished by the durability of its materials, or principles, as by the beauty of its superstructure. It is an emblem of universal *friendship* and benevolence; and instructs us that, in the mind of a Mason, those virtues should be as expansive as the blue arch of heaven itself.

THREE MASTERS OF THE VAILS AS OVERSEERS

Companions: Those who are placed as overseers of any work should be well qualified to judge of its beauties and deformities—its excellencies and defects; they should be capable of estimating the former and amending the latter. This consideration should induce you to cultivate and improve all those qualifications with which you are already endowed, as well as to persevere in your endeavors to acquire those in which you are deficient. Let the various *colors* of the *banners* committed to your charge admonish you to the exercise of the several virtues of which they are emblematic; and you are to enjoin the practice of those virtues upon all who shall present themselves, or the *work* of their hands, for your *inspection*. Let no work receive your approbation but such as is calculated to adorn and strengthen the Masonic edifice. Be industrious and faithful in practicing and disseminating a knowledge of the *true and perfect work*, which alone can stand the test of the *Grand Overseer's Square*, in the great day of trial and retribution. Then, although every *rod* should become a *serpent*, and every serpent an enemy to this institution, yet shall their utmost exertions to destroy its reputation, or sap its foundation, become as impotent as the *leprous hand*, or as *water spilled upon the ground*, which cannot be gathered up again.

CHARGE TO THE TREASURER

Companion: You are elected Treasurer of

this Chapter, and I have the pleasure of invest-
ing you with the badge of your office. The
qualities which should recommend
a Treasurer are *accuracy* and *fidelity;* accuracy in keeping a fair and
minute account of all receipts and
disbursements; fidelity in carefully preserving
all the property and funds of the Chapter, that
may be placed in his hands, and rendering a
just account of the same whenever he is called
upon for that purpose. I presume that your
respect for the institution, your attachment to
the interests of your Chapter, and your regard
for a good name, which is better than precious
ointment, will prompt you to the faithful
discharge of the duties of your office.

CHARGE TO THE SECRETARY

Companion: I with pleasure invest you with
your badge as Secretary of this Chapter. The
qualities which should recommend
a Secretary are *promptitude* in
issuing the notifications and orders
of his superior officers; *punctu-
ality* in attending the meetings of the Chap-

ter; *correctness* in recording their proceedings; *judgment* in discriminating between what is proper and what is improper to be committed to writing; regularity in making his annual returns to the Grand Chapter; integrity in accounting for all moneys that may pass through his hands; and *fidelity* in paying the same over into the hands of the Treasurer. The possession of these good qualities, I presume, has designated you a suitable candidate for this important office; and I cannot entertain a doubt that you will discharge its duties beneficially to the Chapter and honorably to yourself. And when you shall have completed the record of your transactions here below, and finished the term of your probation, may you be admitted into the celestial Grand Chapter of saints and angels, and find your name recorded in the book of life eternal.

CHARGE TO THE CHAPLAIN

E. and Rev. Companion: You are appointed Chaplain of this Chapter; and I now invest you with this jewel, the badge of your office. It is emblematical of eternity, and reminds us that here is not our abiding-place. Your inclination will undoubtedly conspire with your duty when you perform, in the Chapter, those solemn services which created beings should constantly render to their infinite Creator, and which, when offered by one whose holy profession is "to point to heaven, and lead the way," may, by refining our morals, strengthening our virtues, and purifying our minds, prepare us for admission into the society of those above, whose happiness will be as endless as it is perfect.

CHARGE TO THE SENTINEL

Companion: You are appointed Sentinel of this Chapter, and I invest you with the badge 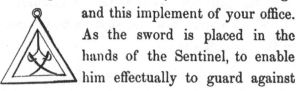 and this implement of your office. As the sword is placed in the hands of the Sentinel, to enable him effectually to guard against the approach of all cowans and eavesdroppers, and suffer none to pass or repass but such as are duly qualified; so it should morally serve as a constant admonition to us to set a guard at the entrance of our thoughts; to place a watch at the door of our lips; to post a sentinel at the avenue of our actions: thereby excluding every unqualified and unworthy thought, word and deed, and preserving consciences void of offense toward God and toward man.

As the first application from visitors for admission into the Chapter is generally made to the Sentinel at the door, your station will often present you to the observation of strangers; it is therefore essentially necessary that he who sustains the office with which you are intrusted should be a man of good morals, steady habits, strict discipline, temperate, affable and discreet. I trust that a just regard for the honor and reputation of the institution will ever induce you to perform with fidelity the trust reposed in you; and when the door of this earthly tabernacle shall be closed, may you find an abundant entrance through the gates into the temple and city of our God.

ADDRESS TO THE HIGH-PRIEST

M. E. Companion: Having been honored with the free suffrages of the members of this Chapter, you are elected to the most important office which it is within their power to bestow. This expression of their esteem and respect should draw from you corresponding sensations; and your demeanor should be such as to repay the honor they have so conspicuously conferred upon you, by an honorable and faithful discharge of the duties of your office. The station you are called to fill is important, not only as it respects the correct practice of our rites and ceremonies, and the internal economy of the Chapter over which you preside, but the public reputation of the institution will be generally found to rise or fall according to the skill, fidelity and discretion with which its concerns are managed, and in proportion as the characters and conduct of its principal officers are estimable or censurable.

You have accepted a trust, to which is attached a weight of responsibility, that will require all your efforts to discharge, honorably to yourself and satisfactorily to the Chapter. You are to see that your officers are capable and faithful in the exercise of their offices. Should they lack ability, you are expected to supply their defects; you are to watch carefully the progress of their performances, and to see that the long-established customs of the institution suffer no derangement in their hands. You are to have a careful eye over the general conduct of the Chapter; see that due order and subordination are observed on all occasions; that the members are properly instructed; that due solemnity be observed in the practice of our rites; that no improper levity be permitted at any time, but more especially at the *introduction of strangers among the workmen.*

In fine, you are to be an example to your officers and members which they need not hesitate to follow; thus securing to yourself the favor of Heaven and the applause of your brethren and companions.

ADDRESS TO THE OFFICERS GENERALLY

Companions in Office: Precept and example should ever advance with equal pace. Those moral duties which you are required to teach unto others you should never neglect to practice yourselves. Do you desire that the demeanor of your equals and inferiors toward you should be marked with deference and respect? Be sure that you omit no opportunity of furnishing them with examples in your own conduct toward your superiors. Do you desire to obtain instruction from those who are more wise or better informed than yourselves? Be sure that you are always ready to impart of your knowledge to those within your sphere who stand in need of and are entitled to receive it. Do you desire distinction among your companions? Be sure that your claims to preferment are founded upon superior attainments; let no ambitious passion be suffered to induce you to envy or supplant a companion who may be considered as better qualified for promotion than yourselves; but rather let a laudable emulation induce you to strive to excel each other in improvement and discipline; ever remembering that he who faithfully performs his duty, even in a subordinate or private station, is as justly entitled to esteem and respect as he who is invested with supreme authority.

ADDRESS TO THE CHAPTER AT LARGE

Companions: The exercise and management

of the sublime degrees of Masonry in your Chapter hitherto are so highly appreciated, and the good reputation of the Chapter so well established, that I must presume these considerations alone, were there no others of greater magnitude, would be sufficient to induce you to preserve and to perpetuate this valuable and honorable character. But when to this is added the pleasure which every philanthropic heart must feel in doing good; in promoting good order; in diffusing light and knowledge; in cultivating Masonic and Christian charity. which are the great objects of this sublime institution, I cannot doubt that your future conduct, and that of your successors, will be calculated still to increase the luster of your justly-esteemed reputation.

May your *Chapter* become *beautiful* as the TEMPLE, *peaceful* as the ARK, and *sacred* as its *most holy place.* May your oblations of *piety* and *praise* be *grateful* as the INCENSE; your love *warm* as its *flame;* and your charity diffusive as its fragrance. May your hearts be *pure* as the ALTAR, and your conduct *acceptable* as the

OFFERING. May the exercise of your CHARITY be as constant as the returning wants of the distressed *widow* and helpless *orphan*. May the approbation of Heaven be your encouragement and the testimony of a good conscience your support. May you be endowed with every good and perfect gift, while *traveling the rugged path of life*, and finally be *admitted within the vail* of heaven, to the full enjoyment of life eternal. So mote it be.—AMEN.

The officers and members of the Chapter will then pass in review in front of the grand officers, with their hands crossed on their breasts, bowing as they pass.

The Grand Captain of the Host then makes the following

PROCLAMATION

In the name of the Most Excellent Grand Chapter of the State of ...., I hereby proclaim .... Chapter, No. ....., to be legally constituted and dedicated, and the officers thereof duly installed.

The grand honors are then given.

Benediction, by the Grand Chaplain.

When the Grand Officers retire, the Chapter will form an advance for them to pass through, and salute them with the grand honors.

CHAPTER JEWELS

High-Priest

King

Scribe

Captain of the Host

Principal Sojourner

R. A. Captain

Masters of the Vails

Treasurer

Secretary

Chaplain

Sentinel

MASONIC DOCUMENTS

Petition for Dispensation for New Chapter.

To the Most Excellent Grand High-Priest of the Grand Chapter of the State of ......:

[Date.]

WE, the undersigned, being Royal Arch Masons in good standing, and having the prosperity of the Royal Craft at heart, are anxious to exert our best endeavors to promote and diffuse the genuine principles of Royal Arch Masonry, and for the convenience of our respective dwellings, and other good reasons, us thereunto moving, we are desirous of forming a new Chapter at ......, in the .... of ......, to be named ...... Chapter.

We, therefore, pray for a Dispensation empowering us to open and hold a regular Chapter at .... aforesaid, and therein to discharge the duties and enjoy the privileges of Royal Arch Masonry, according to the landmarks and usages of the Order, and the constitution and laws of the Grand Chapter.

And we do hereby nominate and recommend Companion A..... B..... to be our first Most Excellent High-Priest; Companion C.... D..... to be our first King, and Companion E..... F... to be our first Scribe.

And should the prayer of this petition be granted, we do hereby promise a strict conformity to the constitution, laws and edicts of the Grand Chapter of the State of ...., *and to the constitution of the General Grand Chapter of the United States,** so far as they may come to our knowledge.

> [This Dispensation must be signed by not less than *nine* Royal Arch Masons.]

It may be presented to either the Grand or Deputy Grand High-Priest, and must be accompanied with the recommendation of the nearest Chapter working under a warrant of constitution, which recommendation should be in the following words:

* These words in italics may be omitted in those States whose Grand Chapters are not in union with the General Grand Chapter.

Form of Recommendation

To the Most Excellent Grand High-Priest of the Grand Chapter of ....:

At a .... convocation of ...... Chapter No. .., holden at ......, on the ... day of ......, A.L. 5 , A. I. 2   -

The petition of several Companions, praying for a Dispensation to open a new Chapter at ......, in the ...... of ...., was duly laid before the Chapter, when it was

Resolved, That this Chapter, being fully satisfied that the petitioners are Royal Arch Masons, in good standing, and being prepared to vouch for their moral character and Masonic abilities, does therefore recommend that the Dispensation prayed for be granted to them.

A true copy of the records.

...., Secretary.

Upon the receipt of this petition, with the accompanying recommendation, the Grand or Deputy Grand High-Priest is authorized to issue his Dispensation, under his private seal, for opening and holding the new Chapter, which Dispensation should be in the following words:

Form of Dispensation for Opening and Holding a New Chapter

To all whom it may concern:

Know ye, that I, ..., Most Excellent Grand High-Priest of the Grand Chapter of the State ......, have received a petition from a constitutional number of Companions, who have been properly vouched for and recommended, which petition sets forth that they are desirous of forming a new Chapter at ......, in the .... of ....; and whereas there appears to me to be good and sufficient cause for granting the prayer of the said petition—

Now, therefore, by virtue of the powers in me vested by the constitutions of the Order, I do hereby grant this my Dispensation, authorizing and empowering Companion A. B. to act as Most Excellent High-Priest; Companion C. D. to act as King, and Companion E. F. to act as Scribe, of a Chapter to be holden at ......, in the .... of ...., to be named and designated as .... Chapter.

And I do hereby further authorize and empower the said Companions, with the necessary assistance, to open and hold Lodges of Mark, Past and Most Excellent Masters, and a Chapter of Royal Arch Masons, and therein to advance, induct, receive and acknowledge

candidates in the several preparatory degrees, and to exalt the
same to the Royal Arch, according to the ancient landmarks and
usages of the Order, and the constitutions of the Grand Chapter
of the State of ......, *and of the General Grand Chapter of the United
States,* but not otherwise.

And this Dispensation shall remain of force until the Grand
Chapter aforesaid shall grant a Warrant of Constitution for the
said Chapter, or until it shall be revoked by me, or by the authority
of the Grand Chapter.

> Given under my hand and seal, at .. ..., this
> ... day of ......, A.L. 5 .., A.I. 2
> ......, *Grand High-Priest.*

At the next convocation of the Grand Chapter this Dispensation
is returned, and the Grand Chapter will, if there be no just reason
to the contrary, grant a Warrant of Constitution, which shall be in
the following language:

Form of a Warrant of Constitution

To all whom it may concern:

The Most Excellent Grand Royal Arch Chapter of ......, assembled in Grand Convocation in the city of ......, and State aforesaid,

Send Greeting:

Know ye, that we, the Grand Royal Arch Chapter of ....., do
hereby authorize and empower our trusty and well-beloved Companions A. B., High-Priest; C. D., King; and E. F., Scribe, to open
and hold a Royal Arch Chapter at ......, in the ...... of ......,
to be known and designated on our register as ..... Chapter, No.
.., and therein to exalt candidates to the august degree of the Holy
Royal Arch, according to the ancient landmarks and usages of
Royal Arch Masonry, and not otherwise.

And we do further authorize and empower our said trusty and
well-beloved Companions, A. B., C. D., and E. F., to open and
hold, under the jurisdiction of the said Chapter, Lodges, and confer the degrees of Mark, Past, and Most Excellent Master, and
therein to advance, induct, receive, and acknowledge candidates,
according to the aforesaid landmarks and usages of the Craft, and
not otherwise.

* These words in italics to be omitted in States not under the jurisdiction of
the General Grand Chapter.

And we do further authorize and empower our said trusty and well-beloved Companions, A. B., C. D., and E. F., to install their successors, duly elected and chosen, to invest them with all the powers and dignities to the offices respectively belonging, and to deliver to them this Warrant of Constitution; and such successors shall, in like manner, from time to time, install their successors, and proceed in the premises as above directed—such installation to be on or before the festival of St. JOHN the Evangelist.

Provided always, that the above-named Companions and their successors do pay and cause to be paid due respect and obedience to the Most Excellent Grand Royal Arch Chapter of ...... aforesaid, and to the edicts, rules, and regulations thereof; otherwise, this Warrant of Constitution to be of no force nor virtue.

> Given in Grand Convocation, under the hands of our Grand officers, and the seal of our Grand Chapter, at ......, this .. day of ......, in the year of light 5 .., and of the discovery 2

G.... H....,   L.... M...., Grand King.
Grand High-Priest.   N.... O...., Grand Scribe.
J.... K....,   [SEAL.]
Deputy G. H. Priest.
        R.... S...., Grand Secretary.

When a Warrant is granted to a new Chapter which is at so great a distance as to render it inconvenient for the Grand officers to personally attend the constitution of the Chapter and the installation of the officers, the Grand High-Priest may issue the following instrument, under his hand and private seal, directed to some Past High-Priest:

Certificate of Proxy, Authorizing a Past High-Priest to Constitute a New Chapter, and to Install its Officers

To all whom it may concern:

But more especially to Companion A. B., Most Excellent High-Priest elect; C. D., King elect; E. F., Scribe elect, and the other Companions who have been empowered by a Warrant of Constitution issued under the authority of the Most Excellent Grand Chapter of ......, to assemble as a regular Chapter at ...... in the ...... of ......, and to be known and designated as .... Chapter, No. ...

Know ye, that, reposing all trust and confidence in the skill,

prudence and integrity of our Most Excellent Companion ......,
I have thought proper—being myself unable to attend—to nominate and appoint the said Most Excellent Companion ...... to
constitute, in form, the Companions aforesaid into a regular
Chapter, and to install the officers elect, according to the ancient
usages of the Craft, and for so doing this shall be his sufficient
warrant.

> Given under my hand and seal, at ......, this
> ... day of ......, in the year of light 5   .,
[SEAL.] and of the discovery 2   ...
>   G...... H......, *Grand High-Priest.*

Petition for the Capitular Degrees

[Date.]

*To the Most Excellent High-Priest, King, Scribe and Companions of
...... Chapter, No. ...:*

The undersigned, a Master Mason, and member of ...... Lodge,
No. ..., under the jurisdiction of the Grand Lodge of ......,
having the good of the Craft at heart, and being desirous of
obtaining further light in Masonry, fraternally offers himself as a
candidate for the degrees conferred in your Chapter. Should his
petition be granted, he promises a cheerful compliance with all the
forms and usages of the Fraternity. His residence is in ......,
and his occupation that of a ......

[Signed]   B...... C......

[To be recommended by two Royal Arch Masons.]

Form of a Demit from a Chapter

To all Royal Arch Masons to whom these presents shall come, greeting:

This is to certify that Companion ...... is, at the date of these
presents, a Royal Arch Mason, in good and regular standing, and
that, having paid all dues, and being free from all charges, he is,
at his own request, by the vote of the Chapter, dismissed· from
membership in ...... Chapter, No. ..., under the jurisdiction of
the Grand Chapter of ......

> Given under my hand and the seal of the Chapter,
> at ...., this .. day of......, in the year of light
[SEAL.] 5 .., and of the discovery 2
>   .... *Secretary.*

Date of Royal Arch Documents

Each of the systems of Masonry has a date peculiar to itself, and which, as referring to some important event in its history, is affixed to its official documents. Thus, the epoch of the creation of light in the beginning of the world, according to the Mosaic cosmogony, has been assumed, for a symbolical reason, as the era of Ancient Craft Masonry, and hence all documents connected with the first three degrees are dated from this period, which date is found by adding 4000 to the vulgar era, and is called in the Year of Light, or *Anno Lucis*, usually abbreviated A∴ L∴—thus the year, 1867, in a Masonic document of the symbolic degrees, would be designated as A∴ L∴ 5867.

Royal Arch Masons use this date also, but in addition to it they commence their peculiar era with the year in which the building of the second Temple was begun, at which time their traditions inform them that a discovery important to the Craft was made. They call their era the Year of the Discovery, or *Anno Inventionis*, sometimes abbreviated A∴ I∴ or *A∴ Inv∴* The second Temple was commenced 530 years before CHRIST, and hence the Royal Arch date is found by adding that number of years to the Christian era. Thus, the present year, 1867, in a Royal Arch document, would be designated as Anno Inventionis 2397, and combining the two Masonic eras, such a document would properly be designated thus: "Anno Lucis 5867, and Anno Inventionis 2397," or "in the Year of Light 5867, and of the Discovery 2397."